BACKYARD BIRD TRACKER

First edition for the United States and Canada published in 2007 by Barron's Educational Series, Inc.

All inquiries should be addressed to:
Barron's Educational Series, Inc.
250 Wireless Boulevard
Hauppauge, NY 11788
www.barronseduc.com

ISBN-13: 978-0-7641-6066-0
ISBN-10: 0-7641-6066-4
Library of Congress Control Number: 2006933441

A Marshall Edition
Conceived, edited, and designed by Marshall Editions
The Old Brewery
6 Blundell Street
London N7 9BH UK

Publisher: Richard Green
Commissioning editor: Claudia Martin
Art direction: Ivo Marloh
Editor: Paul Docherty
Design: Sarah Robson
Indexer: Lynn Bresler
Production: Nikki Ingram

Printed and bound in China by
Midas Printing International Limited
10 9 8 7 6 5 4 3 2 1

BACKYARD BIRD TRACKER

Eastern U.S. Essential Bird-Watcher's Logbook

Rob Hume

BARRON'S

CONTENTS

MAKING THE MOST OF BIRDING

BACKYARD BIRDS CATALOG

BACKYARD BIRD-WATCHER'S LOGBOOK

INTRODUCTION

What is it that draws us to birds? Why is it that watching birds is one of the fastest growing hobbies in the world? There is no single answer, but rather a multitude of answers that are all focused on the bird-human interface: most birds are active when we are active. Their language to us is the language of music—song, percussion, rhythmic, soothing, excited, incredibly varied, yet predictable so that we can identify birds by their voices as we would identify an old friend on the telephone. Birds are often colorful, with each species sporting unique hues and patterns of plumage that allow us to identify it as we might recognize an acquaintance on a busy street.

OUR FINE-FEATHERED FRIENDS

Birds remind us of family and friends by behaviors ranging from the protective attention of parent birds toward their young, to the rambunctious "Feed me! Feed me!" demands of a fledgling, to the bill held high in a face-off of two birds in a territorial dispute at a mutual boundary, to the intimate collaboration of a pair constructing a nest, to the perceived joy in the songs of birds proclaiming the arrival of spring and the beginning of a new cycle of life.

In short we are drawn to birds by their "human" qualities—which, of course, are not human at all, but the perception of our inquisitive minds.

Perhaps we are drawn to birds out of envy—that ability to fly, to soar above the clouds? Or perhaps it is merely the wonder we feel on observing the aerobatics of swallows, the speed of falcons, the effortless soaring of an eagle, the precision flight of a skein of geese or a wheeling flock of hundreds of blackbirds that seems to pulse as if the flock itself were a living being.

We are also drawn to birds by hope. Perhaps it is the hope that they might take advantage of the well-stocked feeder or birdbath we so carefully selected and placed in the garden. Maybe it is the dream that a new species will appear in our yard or that we might find a particular rare bird on a trip to its reported haunts. Or maybe it is the hope we have with the warming days of spring that the birds that nested nearby last year will return.

Perhaps it is the sense of satisfaction, pride, fulfillment, and maybe even the power that we might feel when bluebirds take up residence in the birdhouse we just built and carefully located in our backyard.

Mallards:
These ducks rarely dive into the water for food, preferring to grab morsels on the water's surface.

Perhaps it is our amazement at their arrival back in our yards after hard winters and long migrations. How could we not respect these tiny feathered creatures that dauntlessly withstand snow and storms, heat and drought, and then saucily proclaim their survival with beautiful song. Perhaps it is seeing the awe on a child's face when peering for the first time into a bird nest with eggs or nestlings.

Birds share our lives by contributing to our aesthetic senses and emotional well-being, but they are also, in a sense, our "protectors," consuming insect pests and weed seeds and serving in many ways as barometers of the health of the ecosystems in which we live. Yes, they can be a nuisance. Blackbirds and European Starlings can consume crops and sometimes monopolize our feeders, but they also consume cutworms and other harmful pests. All too often with such birds, we think only of the negative. Proper accounting demands that we look at both sides of the ledger. And we should take a closer look at the ledger of our relationships to birds. We might provide feed and shelter for birds in our yards, but how much of their habitat have we destroyed?

A NEW RELATIONSHIP

This book is a primer for understanding our relationship with birds and their relationship with us. It provides a window on the intimate lives of birds and how they cope with the world in which we both live. Paired with a field guide and a pair of binoculars, this book can open your eyes to a wonderful world that has been there all along, but which so often has gone "unseen." Only once you know what you are looking

Great Spotted Woodpecker:
Its "drumming," usually on dead wood, can be heard up to half a mile away.

at, can you experience it fully. It is the beginning of a beautiful friendship.

The final section of this book provides a log for you to keep track of your explorations and observations of the world of birds. It is a repository for memories, but can also be a well from which you can draw understanding. Record the comings and goings of birds. When did they arrive in spring? When did they build their nest? How many young did they raise? What were they eating? How did they interact with other birds? While we know a great deal about birds, there is much we don't know. Share your discoveries and learn from others. Get involved with a local bird club, Audubon chapter, or regional ornithological society. The wonder of birds and excitement of birding is yours for life.

Jerome A. Jackson (Professor of Biology)
and Bette J. S. Jackson (Associate Professor of Biology)
Florida Gulf Coast University

BIRD LIFE

This chapter reveals the incredible world of birds. The more you know about their world—their struggle for survival, migration patterns, predatory habits—the greater your involvement and enjoyment in bird-watching. Why does a warbler's bill differ so greatly from a macaw's, or the feet of a Harpy Eagle from those of a cormorant? Does plumage change with the seasons? An appreciation of bird anatomy will help you understand why a bird has a particular habitat and prey and has certain behavioral patterns.

WHAT IS A BIRD?

All birds have features in common that, in combination, separate them from other animal groups. Like mammals, they are warm blooded, but like reptiles, they lay eggs, from which their young hatch. Although not all birds fly, most, like bats and millions of species of insects, fly very well. But birds have a unique characteristic: the feather. Birds are clad in thousands of plumes, unlike any other class of animal.

Although the origin of birds remains a talking point, still hotly debated in some circles, most of the fossil evidence, including dromaeosaurs found in China in 2001, shows that birds developed from small, active, warm-blooded, egg-laying dinosaurs. On modern birds, feathers came to replace the scales of reptiles, but grew from the skin in a similar way. How hard, shiny, smooth-edged scales first became feathers is hard to say, but some fossil reptiles have rudimentary or even quite well developed feathers. Perhaps the feathers helped to keep the animal warm, or were used in some sort of ritual display—or even as "nets" to catch prey.

DINOSAUR ORIGINS

Fossils of *Archaeopteryx* clearly show a primitive bird with modern-looking feathers combined with reptilian skull and claws on the front limbs. Some modern birds retain primitive features, such as the remarkable Hoatzin, which lives in the forests of South America. This strange bird still has sharp, curved claws on the fore edge of its wings, which it uses to clamber through twigs and foliage soon after leaving the nest.

All birds have a skeleton that recalls that of reptiles, with a strong backbone of many vertebrae, a pelvis that supports the hind limbs, and "arms" much like ours in bone structure. The larger bones of flying birds are hollow, with a

Early bird: One of the world's most famous fossils, Archaeopteryx *has many of the features of a small dinosaur, with a long bony tail and toothed jaws. Wings and flight feathers, however, suggest that it was a bird and could fly.*

TWO OF A FEATHER

Feathers ensure that no bird can be taken for any other class of creature once it is seen well, although the tight plumes of a penguin may look more like fur than feathers. Similarly, no other creature is often mistaken for a bird, despite the "beak" of a Duck-billed Platypus and the flight of a bat. Only the Hummingbird Hawk-moth and its relatives, which are found in Europe, are regularly mistaken for real hummingbirds by the inexperienced.

network of crossbars to give maximum strength combined with minimum weight. Birds' lungs and the surrounding bones are interlinked in such a way that the bird is able to extract oxygen from the air both while inhaling and exhaling (see Bird Anatomy, pp. 14–15), and this unique arrangement makes their respiration extremely efficient. Their high oxygen intake allows birds the very high metabolic rates they require to convert food to energy, which they use very rapidly in their energy-demanding lives.

BEGINNINGS OF FLIGHT

It is possible to imagine how birds first took to the air, but it is still a debated subject. Did they run along the ground to gain speed, flapping their wings until they took off, or did they climb up trees and rocks to get sufficient height to glide from place to place? The latter seems most likely. Even now, flying snakes, flying squirrels, and other creatures that glide rather than fly gain height by climbing, then move by leaping into the air and sailing forward

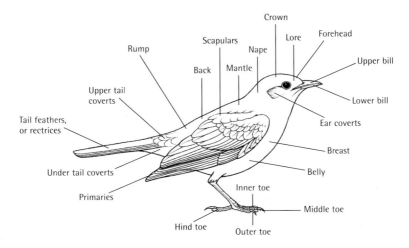

External features: The external features of a bird helps us understand its underlying structure and are also used for identification in the field.

and downward, using some sort of aerodynamic device, such as a flap of skin between the fore and hind limbs—just like a paper glider—to navigate. Birds developed long, stiff feathers on their forelimbs—wings—and turned flight into a fine art. Powered flight required the development of a deep breastbone, to which are attached the pectoral muscles that beat the wings.

AVIAN SENSES
Eyesight
Most birds have excellent sight and see as well as humans; some have a greater ability to define detail. Eyesight is very poor in a few

Barn Owl: Owls combine special eyesight adaptations with exceptional hearing.

species, such as the Kiwi of New Zealand, and this is compensated for by a highly developed sense of smell. Birds probably see a wider range of color than humans do. Owls, however, forego good color vision, but see better than most other birds in very low levels of light, although they cannot see in complete darkness.

Hearing
Birds have very good hearing and some, such as owls, can use it more precisely than we can, for example to pinpoint the sounds made by their prey, even in the dark. Some owls, such as the Barn Owl, have asymmetric ears, both in terms of size and shape as well as their position on the head, so that the tiny sound of a mouse rustling in dead leaves, or even pattering in a tunnel deep beneath snow, can be narrowed down to within less than a degree by the minutely differing sounds picked up by each ear. This is why owls use such engaging actions, twisting and bobbing their heads as if incurably curious: they are simply getting a better aural fix, like turning a satellite dish or television aerial to get the best reception.

Ruby-throated Hummingbird:
This bird has remarkable
senses that allow it to perform
aerobatic feats, but it probably
has poor hearing and little
sense of taste.

Smell

Not all birds have a good sense of smell, but some do and they use it well. Some vultures can smell dead animals lying invisibly on the forest floor and are followed down by other species, which cannot detect the scent. Some seabirds, such as island-nesting petrels that come ashore only at night to avoid predators, locate their nests using smell. In the same way, colonial birds can locate their own chicks in a dense group by homing in on their uniquely different calls.

Taste

Few birds seem to have a strongly developed sense of taste. Nevertheless, some foods are clearly distasteful: hence the value of warning colors for some insects, plants, and even other birds, which reduce predation by indicating a nasty taste, or even a poison. It is likely, then, that some birds at least find certain foods to be more pleasant tasting than others.

THE RHYTHM OF LIFE

Birds are driven by the need to survive and reproduce. They must find food, safe roosting sites and good places to nest, and a mate. They feel pain and fear and much of their behavior is based on avoiding injury or death. The colors and patterns of many birds' plumage are dictated by similar factors: some have become masters in the art of camouflage, others are gaudily colored to help them attract mates and outdo rivals.

BIRD ANATOMY

Birds exhibit a wide range of biological adaptations that distinguish them from other animals; many of these are geared toward flight, the single most distinguishing feature of birds. The anatomy of flying birds is a superb example of the compromise between structural strength and low weight that is needed to achieve efficient flight. Other adaptations help different birds survive in their particular habitat.

In common with other warm-blooded vertebrates (animals with backbones) such as mammals, birds have a rigid, bony skeleton that supports and protects the soft tissues and organs within the rib cage and provides anchorage for the muscles.

THE SKELETON
Bird skeletons, however, have evolved from the heavy structures of their reptilian ancestors into much lighter, but sturdier, frameworks. The larger bones of flying birds are hollow and reinforced with a network of crossbars—like the truss on a bridge, this structure combines great strength with low weight, giving the bird a low take-off weight and a high power-to-weight ratio, which is vital for efficient flight (see Flight, pp. 20–23). Besides being hollow, many bird bones are fused together, which reduces flexibility, but greatly increases strength in order to resist the great forces birds experience during flight, especially during take-off and landing.

HEAD
A bird's head is small, with lightweight, cavity-filled skull bones, and typically very large round orbits, or eye sockets. Their toothless jaws, which are the

foundation of the beak, vary greatly in shape according to the specific, often diet-related, tasks for which these tools are needed (see Birds' Bills, p. 26, and Birds' Feet, p. 30). The underside of the lower jaw consists of a soft throat pouch, or gular region, which is little developed in birds such as sparrows and finches, more obvious in some, such as cormorants, and most evident in the remarkable extensible pouch of the pelicans. The upper bill has openings for the nostrils, usually close to the base. The lower bill allows little or no sideways, or chewing, movement. In many birds, especially swifts, nightjars, and other insect-eaters, the bill is relatively small but the mouth, or gape, is very wide.

SPINE, PELVIS, AND LEGS
The "wishbone" consists of two clavicles, or collarbones, fused together to act as a strengthening strut that braces the wings apart. Flightless birds and some others, such as the parrots, have a greatly reduced wishbone. A bird's neck varies greatly among species in length and mobility, but in all birds, the bones of the spine are mostly fused together to form a solid, rigid unit that is firmly attached to the large pelvic girdle. The pelvic bones are also

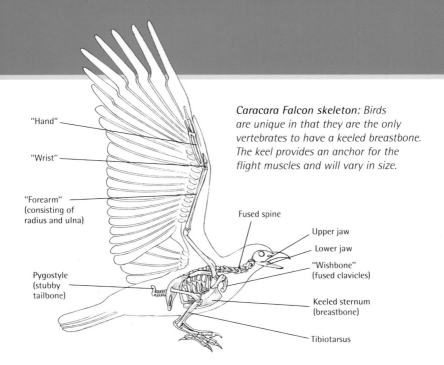

"Hand"

"Wrist"

"Forearm"
(consisting of
radius and ulna)

Pygostyle
(stubby
tailbone)

*Caracara Falcon skeleton: Birds
are unique in that they are the only
vertebrates to have a keeled breastbone.
The keel provides an anchor for the
flight muscles and will vary in size.*

Fused spine

Upper jaw

Lower jaw

"Wishbone"
(fused clavicles)

Keeled sternum
(breastbone)

Tibiotarsus

fused, and act with the rigid spine to distribute the weight of the body during landing. The lightweight leg bones are operated by powerful muscles on the upper leg, but only by tendons on the lower leg—this sturdy, compact structure acts as a shock absorber during landing. Birds' feet vary greatly in size and form, playing vital roles in locomotion and feeding (*see* Bills and Feet, pp. 26–31).

BREAST AND WINGS

The breastbone, or sternum, varies from family to family; in gliding birds it is smaller, but in those with powerful, deep wingbeats, such as pigeons, it is large and has a prominent ridge, or keel. The relatively massive breast muscles, or pectorals, attach to the keel, which provides a deep anchorage for the powerful downward sweep of the wings made by contracting the pectorals. The wing is reminiscent of a mammal's arm or forelimb, but with variations: the upper arm is generally

embedded in the body or hidden beneath the body feathers. The "inner wing" corresponds to the human forearm (the radius and ulna) and the outer wing, beyond the "wrist," to the "hand," which has several fused digits but a separate thumb (*see* Feathers, pp. 16–19).

RESPIRATORY SYSTEM

Birds have developed a highly specialized respiratory and circulatory system that allow them to metabolize oxygen and other substances rapidly so that vast amounts of energy can be generated—relative to their size—to power their wings. Air first passes into the lungs, and then farther into extensions of the lungs called air sacs that reach into the bird's hollow bones, before passing out through the lungs again, allowing the bird to take oxygen on each passage. A bird's heart also beats very rapidly to move the oxygen: a hummingbird has up to 1,000 heartbeats a minute during flight.

FEATHERS

A feather is an amazing structure. It is made of keratin, a hornlike substance that also forms the basis of our fingernails. It is lightweight, yet strong and durable—essential structural requirements for a bird to achieve flight. Feathers grow from tiny follicles arranged in tracts in the skin; they are regularly shed and replaced.

Each feather has a main shaft, or rachis, from which extends a "vane" on each side, consisting of scores of small, interlinked branches called barbs. The base of the shaft is hollow to maximize strength and minimize weight. Together, these make up the basic leaflike shape of the whole feather.

ZIPPED TOGETHER

The barbs are held together in a complex series of indentations and hooks called barbules, which interlink in a similar way to Velcro. If the barbules become detached, the feather appears disarranged and ragged. Birds preen

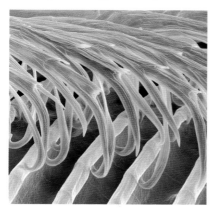

Barbules: Feathers have a brilliant hook-fastener construction, with thousands of tiny hooks clinging to minute stays.

regularly every day, each one spending long periods of time gently but firmly sliding its feathers one by one through its bill. This action removes any debris from the feather, zips the barbs together again, and keeps them in good shape.

Flight feathers are stiff and usually slightly curved. Smaller feathers tend to be wider, rounder, and less rigid, especially at the base, where some of the vane is composed of loose and wispy barbs. These barbs at the base of the shaft are almost entirely lacking the barbules that zip the rest of the feather together. They create a soft, down-like layer that insulates against both heat and cold.

THE MAIN FEATHER TRACTS

The covering of feathers on a bird is called its plumage. If you spread a bird's wing, you will see that the feathers are arranged in neat zones. Forming the wingtip are large, long, stiff feathers that grow from the fused "fingers" of the "hand"—these are the primary feathers and are of different lengths. Along the trailing edge of the inner half of the wing are the secondary feathers, which are also stiff but shorter than the primaries. These grow from the "forearm." Just beyond the bend of the wing—the wrist, or carpal joint—is the bird's "thumb," from which grows a small tuft of feathers that can be raised from the main surface of the wing in flight. This is called the "alula," or bastard wing. The alula is important in helping a bird maneuver in the air at low speeds, and it has long been emulated in aircraft designs.

Each of the main tracts of flight feathers of the wings and tail is covered at its base by a row of smaller feathers—the coverts, which cover the gaps at the base of the flight feathers, creating a smooth, solid surface for efficient flight. The contour feathers on the bird's body are less obviously, yet still precisely, arranged, cloaking the body to give it its streamlined shape. There are areas of a bird's body that are less defined by feather tracts than by color and pattern, such as the forehead, crown, nape, cheeks, breast, and flank.

Eagle wing: The "fingered" wingtip feathers of soaring birds taper toward the tip and curve upward under pressure from the bird's weight against the air beneath; the outermost feather curves most. "Slots" between the feathers reduce turbulence and increase stability.

WEAR AND TEAR
Feathers gradually become ragged and lose color. The pigments that provide most of the colors in plumage (*see* Colors and Patterns, pp. 32-37) fade with age, especially if they are exposed to strong sun or saltwater. These exposed parts become paler and duller while the base, usually covered by other feathers, remains bright and fresh. Some pigments, such as the dark-colored melanin, give feathers added strength.

MOLT
Feathers, once grown, are dead structures that gradually wear and deteriorate. To counteract this, birds molt their feathers regularly, shedding

WING ANATOMY
The main tracts of flight feathers on a bird's wings, such as the primaries and secondaries, are overlapped by the coverts—various series of smaller feathers that merge with the main tracts to form an aerodynamic surface.

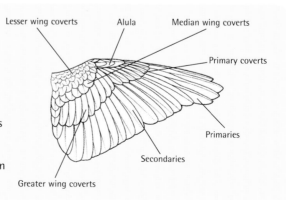

Lesser wing coverts
Alula
Median wing coverts
Primary coverts
Primaries
Secondaries
Greater wing coverts

and replacing them symmetrically, and usually a few at a time, to maintain maximum efficiency. Some ducks and geese, however, drop all their flight feathers at once and are unable to fly until new ones grow. Most birds, though, shed their feathers one by one in a regular, fixed sequence—on larger birds you can easily observe it happening. Watch flying birds and look for gaps in the shape of the wing, or for new, fresh, dark feathers growing among paler, rough-edged, old ones.

Birds have a tough time during summer as they search for food for themselves and their young: they push through foliage in innumerable visits to their nests; some live in abrasive beach environments; many are constantly exposed to damaging rays from the sun; and all face the rigors of courtship and defending a territory. Their feathers take a battering and become dull and pale. As a result, most birds undergo a

Lapland Longspur: The winter male (top) has his pattern broken up by pale feather tips. These fade away in spring to reveal his full summer finery (bottom).

post-breeding molt in late summer and autumn, emerging as fresh and bright as ever in a new set of feathers.

Replacing feathers consumes a lot of energy, and molt must therefore occur when energy-rich foods are readily available and when the bird is not involved in other energy-sapping activities. It is no accident that the

Mallards: This pair are in perfect breeding plumage in late winter; by summer, the male will have changed to a color much more like that of his mate.

ALL WORN OUT

Some species use wear instead of molting to change color, avoiding an energy-intensive change of feathers. The Eurasian Starling, for example, acquires fresh, glossy feathers in fall, each of which has a white tip. The winter plumage is then spotted. By spring, however, as the breeding season approaches, the white tips have worn off and the bird is a beautiful, glossy black all over. In North America, the same thing happens to the Eastern Meadowlark. In fall, they acquire new yellow breast feathers that are tipped with tan. As a result, they blend in with dried winter grasses. By spring, the tan tips have worn away to reveal the bird's beautiful, bright-yellow breast.

complete annual molt of birds occurs after breeding and usually before migration. The timing of molt is important, especially to migrant birds. Some, such as the Common Tern, have a partial molt in autumn before they migrate south, which is completed by another partial molt in their wintering areas. The Arctic Tern molts later, after its migration. Large birds of prey, in contrast, may molt almost continually, replacing a few feathers here and there at almost any time. Their flight feathers (the big wing feathers that affect their ability to fly), however, are shed and replaced in a strict sequence.

The female of some birds of prey, such as harriers, molt some of their flight feathers while they are incubating their eggs and being fed by their mate. Others wait until they have reared their young to molt—when watching kites, it is sometimes possible to identify pairs that have failed to hatch eggs or rear chicks, because they can begin their molt earlier than those that are still feeding a family.

Not only does molting refresh a bird's plumage, it can also change a bird's appearance according to age and season. Dull-brown young birds, for example, become brighter as they gain adult feathers. Drab winter plumage can be changed for brighter breeding plumages. It is not always so simple: ducks, for example, pair up in winter and look brightest in the coldest months. In summer, the male loses his ability to fly and molts into a faded, dark pattern—called "eclipse" plumage—so that he is more camouflaged and less likely to fall prey to a passing hawk or fox.

Herring Gull: The white wingtip spots wear away in summer. The black areas fade with long exposure to sunlight.

FLIGHT

Most birds fly, although there are exceptions. Some very large birds, such as rheas, Emus, and Ostriches—the ratites—are too big and heavy to make flight practical and have become flightless. Others, such as penguins covered in a thick layer of heavy blubber, cannot fly in air but have adapted to swim expertly in water. Some birds live on isolated islands and have lost the ability to fly due to the absence of natural predators. Nevertheless, most birds take to the air.

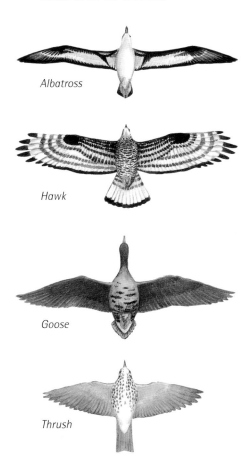

Albatross

Hawk

Goose

Thrush

Different birds have different methods of leaving the ground to fly. Most birds are powerful enough to fly up from level ground or water, using muscular legs to leap upward and a strong downbeat of the wings to gain lift.

BECOMING AIRBORNE

Small birds can burst into flight with ease, but larger ones, such as geese, need more effort and often begin with a running takeoff. Others, such as vultures, take advantage of rising air currents of thermals or winds deflected upwards by ridges and simply open large wings to be carried upward.

Others simply drop from a height, spreading their wings to begin flight. Seabirds living on sheer cliffs use this method to leave their ledges and fly, losing height before their wings provide enough lift and forward momentum to keep them airborne. Many birds of prey sit on high perches and sail out into the open air, using wind and warm, rising air to give them lift. Albatrosses, swans, many ducks, and other heavy birds have

Wing shapes: A bird's wing shape and size are directly related to its flight.

CONTROLLING FLIGHT

Birds use their wings and tail to control their flight. The short wings and long tail of an accipiter—a type of hawk—allow it to twist and turn through trees; the long wings of a kite let it glide over open ground while its tail twists and tilts to produce precise movement. In tight situations, such as landing on a perch or ledge, the tail is spread to act as a brake, the bastard wing lifts to regulate airflow over the wing and prevent a stall, and the feet are lowered, too, to aid balance and add extra drag to reduce speed.

a "takeoff run," from land or water, by beating their wings and rushing forward until they gain enough momentum to take to the air.

UNDERWAY

Once aloft, birds use their wings to stay in flight. Small songbirds have rapid wingbeats, often interspersed with brief pauses that give characteristic "flitting" movements. Longer pauses between bursts of wing beats create the familiar rising and falling—undulating—flight of finches and buntings.

A bird's wingtip feathers have a narrow outer vane and a broad inner vane that flex around the stiff shaft as they are pushed through the air. As the wings beat up and down, these asymmetric feathers act as tiny "propellers" that give forward motion. As the surface of the wing pushes against air, it keeps the bird airborne.

The wings of both small and large birds have an airfoil shape that helps them gain lift, and the force of the wing beating against the air gives them forward motion. The upper surface of the wing bulges upward—it is convex—while the under surface is flatter

or even concave. Thus, as the bird moves forward, the shape of its wing, just like that of an aircraft, forces air to travel farther over the top of the wing than underneath, increasing its speed and reducing its pressure compared with the shorter airflow beneath: this gives "lift," causing the bird to rise. Birds with strongly concave wings, such as herons and egrets, have better control at slow speeds. They cannot fly fast, but land gently to protect their long, delicate legs. Those with less concave wings, such as many ducks, can fly fast, depend

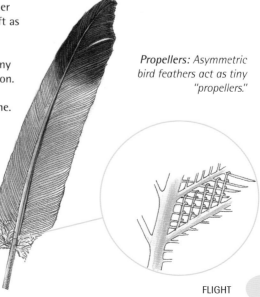

Propellers: Asymmetric bird feathers act as tiny "propellers."

on the cushioning impact of water, and require very large flight muscles. Falcons, with less concave wings, have the speed they need to pursue prey, but lack the ability to fly slowly. As a bird moves forward, it must gain sufficient lift to counteract its natural tendency to fall, perfectly balancing its long "dive" with the aerodynamic forces that keep it aloft.

It achieves forward momentum as a result of a delicate balance of the aerodynamic properties of its wing and tail structure, the power of its muscles, and its needs for slow or fast flight, direct flight in the open, or high maneuverability in capturing prey or moving through forested habitats.

DYNAMIC AND THERMAL SOARING

Long-traveling seabirds such as albatrosses and shearwaters have long, narrow wings that are ideal for gliding. They are able to rise against the wind, keel over to catch the breeze and sail downwind over long distances without a wingbeat. They then turn to rise again and repeat the process. They use the air currents rising off the tops of steep-sided waves. In this way, they travel for hours with scarcely a wingbeat. In calm air, however, they must use a lot of effort to fly. They do not have the powerful muscles needed to beat their big wings for long periods.

Big birds over land take advantage of thermals to soar. When rocks, bare earth, or even urban areas become warm in the

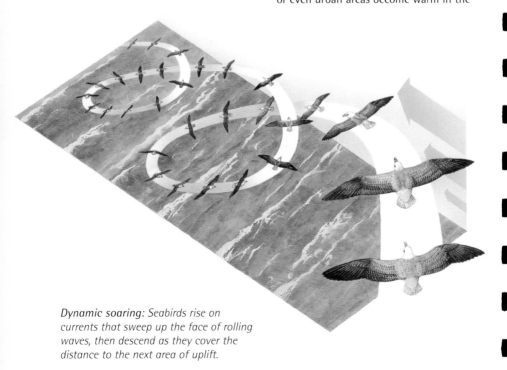

Dynamic soaring: Seabirds rise on currents that sweep up the face of rolling waves, then descend as they cover the distance to the next area of uplift.

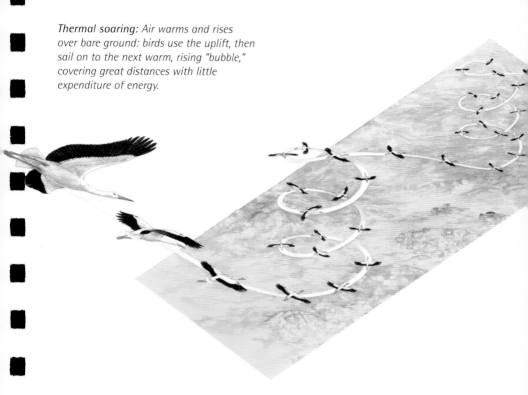

Thermal soaring: Air warms and rises over bare ground: birds use the uplift, then sail on to the next warm, rising "bubble," covering great distances with little expenditure of energy.

sun, the air above these areas heats up and rises like steam from a tea kettle. Birds use such rising warm air to gain great heights with little expenditure of energy. They can then glide in whatever direction they wish, balancing gravity and lift, and slowly losing height until they have to circle upward again. In this way, birds such as vultures can search for food all day long with ease, and storks, many hawks, and cranes can make huge migratory flights with minimum energy expenditure. The one problem with this type of flying is that it does not work over the sea, where the air does not form thermals. Migrating flocks must find the narrowest possible sea crossings in spring and autumn.

SHORT, STRAIGHT, AND FAST

Large, bulky birds, such as turkeys, pheasants, grouse, and similar species cannot glide great distances, nor make long migratory flights, nor twist or turn in intricate aerobatics. They have big, meaty breast muscles—pectorals—attached to a deep breastbone. These muscles allow brief bursts of deep, fast, powerful wingbeats. They can fly off straight and fast when disturbed, but run out of energy very quickly and have to land again, continuing their escape on foot.

EYES AND VISION

Most birds perceive a similar range of colors and amount of detail as do humans. Some species, however, see a wider spectrum of light and this ability may be more widespread than we think. Those species whose eyes see less color than ours are more sensitive to shapes and movement in poor light than we are.

SEEING SIDEWAYS

Our eyes are forward-facing and work together—the field of view of each eye overlaps the field of view of the other. Such vision is called "binocular" and the slight variations in perspective it affords allow us to judge size and distance. Some birds have their eyes on the sides of the head and have limited binocular vision as a result. Each eye sees a wide field of view that is separate from the other. This is hard for us to comprehend, but the result is that these birds can detect motion—such as the approach of a predator—from almost any direction. They cannot, however, be certain of its size or the distance of the movement's source. Some birds, such as woodcocks, can even see behind them, having complete all-around vision. This is ideal for spotting potential danger from behind while probing for food in front.

Most birds, though, have a fairly wide field of binocular vision. This is vital for pinpointing position and judging distance. Such judgments are crucial for birds that fly from perch to perch within the confines of a bush or tree, for instance, or any bird that catches mobile prey.

Owls and birds of prey have forward-facing eyes that give binocular vision over about 90 degrees; human eyes give about 120 degrees. Gannets, herons, egrets, and others have a similarly invaluable band of vision covered by both eyes, giving them a good fix on their prey. Close one eye and try to put a fingertip on a small object and you will see how critical vision with two eyes is when trying to make precise judgments.

THE EYES OF AN OWL

Owls have binocular vision. Their eyes are as large as ours but are more tubular than round, giving them a larger image on the retina and increasing visual sharpness. Some species' eyes are about 100 times more sensitive than ours. In poor light, the human eye sees more on the periphery of its field of view than it does straight ahead, detecting movement and shape rather than color and detail. Owls' eyesight is similar to this right across their field of view, even in daylight: they see little color and little detail and are long-sighted. But in low light levels they are much better than us at detecting shapes and movements.

ACUTE VISION

Birds of prey have exceptionally sharp sight and are able to resolve much detail. With the vision of a falcon, we could read small print from 83 feet (25 m); an eagle's eyes would allow us to see a rabbit from two miles (3 km); and some hawks can see a grasshopper against a green background from 640 feet (200 m).

This exceptionally sharp sight is possible because of a layer called the retina at the rear of the eyeball. In birds of prey, the retina is very large and equipped with a vast number of light receptors, called rods and cones. Our eye has about 200,000 cones per square millimeter of retina, while an eagle's has about 1 million. These are perfect for picking out minute detail, rather like millions of pixels in a digital picture.

Two special organs aid acute vision. Like humans, birds have a central area called the fovea that surrounds the optic nerve and has extra dense rods and cones to pick up additional light. Birds of prey also have a second,

Hovering kestrel: Some birds of prey see ultraviolet light, enabling them to detect urine trails and droppings left by rodents.

peripheral fovea, which gives them greater acuity over a wider field of view. Another adaptation is the pecten, a compact assemblage of capillaries that is especially well developed in birds of prey. It provides nourishment to the eye without the degree of visual disruption caused by the eye capillaries of other animals, which spread throughout the eye and scatter light.

BROAD SPECTRUM

Unlike humans, pigeons and kestrels can see ultraviolet light. Kestrels use this sense to detect rodent feces and urine, which are visible in ultraviolet, allowing the bird to pick out rodent trails by the ultraviolet beacons of their droppings. Pigeons use their ultraviolet sight to detect edible seeds on the ground, against which the seeds clearly stand out.

Another feature of birds' eyes, which they have in common with many other animals, is the nictitating membrane, also known as the third eyelid. This moves horizontally across the eyeball and is used to remove debris and keep water out, while also giving protection against injury from an adversary. In many aquatic birds, the nictitating membrane is transparent and functions like swim goggles to enhance their vision under water.

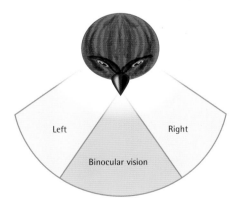

Binocular vision: Forward-facing eyes give a wide field of vision in which objects are seen by both eyes, which helps the bird pinpoint their precise position.

Left

Right

Binocular vision

BIRDS' BILLS

The bills of birds occur in a tremendous range of shapes, reflecting the adaptation of each species to its unique mode of obtaining food. Many birds also have specially shaped or colored bills that they use in courtship rituals.

Common Raven: The raven uses its heavy, arched, powerful bill for all-round foraging and tearing up tough items before eating.

Icterine Warbler: Shallow but broad, this bird's bill is shaped for seizing insects.

Channel-billed Toucan: This bird has a remarkable bill, which is very large but extremely lightweight, for reaching fruits on thin twigs.

A bird's bill consists of an upper jaw, which is fixed on the skull and almost immobile, and a lower jaw that is articulated like ours and opens to reveal a wide gape.

HORNLIKE SHEATHS
Each jaw has a bony base. The lower base is formed by two bones, which are fused together where they meet near the tip of the bill. The space between them is filled by the soft throat and chin (or sometimes a fleshy pouch). These bones are covered by hard, hornlike—or sometimes leathery—sheaths that give the bill its detailed shape.

On a few birds, such as the puffin, the sheaths are shed or modified after the breeding season, allowing for marked differences in the size of the bill, according to the season. In most birds, seasonal changes are limited to alterations in color. On birds such as herons, these color changes can be brief but rapid, with a visible increase in the intensity of color during periods of excitement in spring courtship.

FLEXIBLE BILLS
While the upper jaw is fixed, the tip of the long upper jaw extending from the skull can be surprisingly flexible. Even birds such as cormorants can raise the upper bill to an unexpected degree in a wide "yawn." Snipe and woodcock have especially sensitive bills, and they can detect prey while probing deep

in soft mud or soil. Once a worm has been found, by touch, the bill is flexible enough to allow the tip to open and grasp the prey, which can then be swallowed without a pause in the deep probing.

SEED-EATERS' BILLS

Sparrows and finches have broad, deep, triangular bills for feeding on hard seeds. They vary, nevertheless. A goldfinch has a fine, pointed, triangle-shaped bill for probing into complex flower heads such as thistles for seeds. The bill of a crossbill is literally crossed at the tip, which allows it to reach inside of the scales of pine and larch cones to extract the seeds within with its tongue. Most finches have "middle-sized" triangular bills for crushing tough seeds, and their bills have sharp cutting edges to de-husk them. At a feeder you can often watch a finch manipulating a seed with its bill and tongue, peeling off the outer husk and nibbling at the kernel within.

INSECT-EATERS' FINE TOOLS

Insect-eating birds such as warblers have fine, narrow bills for picking tiny prey from twigs and foliage. Flycatchers have broader bills, often fringed with stiff bristles, and wide mouths so they can catch insects in flight. Swifts and nightjars have minute bills, but huge mouths, which open wide to catch insects in the air. But many birds have "all rounder" bills, and even sparrows can catch insects when they wish to, and scoop up vast numbers of aphids when feeding their young.

    Starlings have stout, strong, pointed bills with especially adapted muscles that they use to probe into grass and open their bills to get at the larvae of

Green Woodpecker: The dagger-shaped, chisel-like bill of this bird is used for digging into ant-hills and chipping out nesting cavities in tree branches.

Northern Cardinal: This bird has a thick, triangular, seed-eater's bill.

Blue-and-yellow Macaw: The deep, arched, hook-tipped bill of this bird is used to rip open fruits and seed pods.

Golden Eagle: Typical for a bird of prey, this eagle has a hooked bill, which is used for tearing apart meaty foods.

Giant Hummingbird: This bill is specialized for taking nectar from flowers and snatching tiny insects.

Common Redshank: The slim, sensitive bill of this bird can probe into wet mud and sand.

chafers and other prey. A thrush has a stronger bill than a warbler, and it is longer and more slender than a sparrow's: they eat worms, grubs, seeds, and all kinds of fruit. Its bill is more of a tool for all trades than a specialized instrument.

HOOKED AND TOOTHED BILLS

Birds of prey have a hook-tipped bill, also known as a beak, for tearing prey apart. Few of these birds capture prey in their beak—they normally use their feet to snatch their victims—but many kill prey with a sharp bite. A falcon's beak has a small "tooth" on the sheath of the upper bill to help sever the neck of a mouse or small bird. Vultures have bills that are designed for the food in their local area: the big Black and Griffon Vultures (true members of the Falconiformes) of Europe have heavy bills that can tear into the hide of dead animals, while the Turkey Vulture of the Americas (related to storks) and the Egyptian Vulture of southern Europe (another Falconiform bird) have narrow, fine bills for probing deep inside carcasses made of weaker tissue.

Other birds also have hooked bills. Parrots are primarily fruit and seed eaters, and their thick, hooked bills allow them to cope with large fruit and seed pods. Mergansers not only have hooks, but also tooth-like edges to the bill, to keep a firm grip on slippery, muscular fish. Gannets, kingfishers, herons, and egrets manage to eat their fish diet quite well without either feature, grasping prey in their powerful, pointed, sharp-edged bills before turning them to swallow the fish head-first so there is no risk of choking on extended spines or fins.

PROBES AND HAMMERS

Shorebird bills are greatly adapted to habitat and food preferences. Curlews have down-curved bills, perhaps so they can easily see what they are doing with the bill's fine tip. But they also probe and twist the bill, and the curve might allow them a better chance to detect prey. Godwits, snipe, and dowitchers, however, probe adequately with long, straight bills.

Plovers take food from the shore, often on mudflats, using a shorter, thicker bill; a Dunlin picks from, or just beneath, the surface of mud and sand with a longer, fine-tipped bill. A turnstone has a strong, slightly up-curved bill that it uses to move pebbles and seaweed in search of hidden invertebrates. An avocet's up-curved bill is swept sideways through shallow water to capture prey near the surface, while a spoonbill's broad bill with its wide, flattened tip is swept—slightly open—from side to side through the water until a fish is touched and the bill grabs it as with a pair of salad tongs.

Oystercatchers can have a pointed bill, used to slip inside shellfish to cut the muscle that holds the shells tight together, or a blunt-tipped bill, which is used to hammer the shells to pieces.

Red-breasted Merganser: With serrated edges for grasping fish, this is a typical sawbill duck's bill.

Mallard: This bird uses its broad bill for "dabbling" in shallow water to pick up seeds and aquatic creatures.

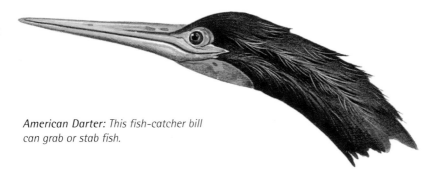

American Darter: This fish-catcher bill can grab or stab fish.

BIRDS' FEET

Birds rely not only on their wings to get around—they use their feet for walking. Their feet are adapted for walking styles as well as for gripping tasks, whether it be an eagle snatching a fish or a robin perching in a tree.

Common Pheasant: The strong, stubby feet of this bird are adapted for walking.

Carrion Crow: This bird has strong feet adapted for perching and walking.

Northern Jacana: The exceptionally long toes of the jacana help to spread its weight on floating leaves.

Rock Ptarmigan: Feathered toes give this bird better insulation in snow.

Most birds have four toes, three pointing forward and one backward, to allow for a good grip on a perch, such as a twig or branch. Small songbirds that walk or run on the ground, such as larks and pipits, have a very long hind claw. Some larger birds that walk or run in open places have only three toes, with the hind toe lost or reduced to a stub.

The hind toe is also much reduced in ducks, geese, swans, and gulls; instead, the front three toes are joined by leathery webs that give a stronger push against water for more powerful swimming. Gannets, pelicans, cormorants, and their relatives reveal their close relationship by their feet, on which broad webs join all four toes.

Falcons have strong toes and sharp, arched claws, with which they grasp their prey. Bird-eating harriers and hawks have longer legs, much longer toes, and needle-sharp, curved claws that enable them to capture birds in flight and kill them by puncturing vital organs.

Green Woodpecker: The outer toe of this species splays outward and backward to give good grip on a rounded branch.

WADERS

Shorebirds may have very long legs for wading in shallow water. Plovers have just three toes, while sandpipers have four, longer, more slender toes. Avocet toes are joined by partial webs. Similarly, rails and crakes may have very long, slim toes to take their weight on soft mud and floating vegetation—yet the closely related coots have broad lobes along each side of each toe, as do the grebes. These fold flat when the foot is pushed forward through water, reducing drag, but open out as the foot is pushed back, to give forward thrust.

House Sparrow: Typical for perching birds, the sparrow has three toes pointing forward and one back.

American Harpy Eagle: Its huge feet, strong toes, and arched, sharp claws enable this bird to kill large prey such as monkeys.

Great Cormorant: All four toes of this bird are joined by webs to provide powerful underwater propulsion.

Black Coot: The lobes on this bird's toes spread out on back stroke and fold away on forward stroke for efficient swimming.

Grey Heron: Its long legs and toes allow this heron to wade in the shallows and stand on soft mud without sinking.

Ostrich: Its feet are designed for long-distance walking and running at great speed.

COLORS AND PATTERNS

Feathers occur in just about any color variation you can think of: they may be solid in color, striped lengthwise, barred across, spotted, criss-crossed with blocks of color, mottled, smoothly graded, and so on. Their patterns and colors can be amazingly complex. Yet many birds have a basic similarity, especially within families. For example, gulls are gray, white, and black, many hawks have barred undersides, many falcons have dark mustache-like marks, and many ducks have colorful hind wing patches.

REMARKABLE CONSISTENCY

If you look at 10,000 Black-headed Gulls at a reservoir roost, there will be almost no variation among them in the color of their upperparts: all are the same pale, silvery-gray. Watch the thrushes in your garden and, year after year, they will each have exactly the same shade of brown on the back. There are individual differences, but the essential truth is that birds of one species are usually amazingly alike.

This helps bird-watchers, because it makes the birds easier to identify. Variation within a species is often linked to geography. When one species has a wide geographic range, those at one end can be a little—or, rarely, a lot—different from those at the other. In many geographically variable species, there is a smooth gradient of variation (such as in size or color) from one extreme of the range to another. Such a smooth gradient is called a "cline."

Northern Shoveler: There is no discernible difference between the shades of rusty-red, dark green, brown, and blue on shovelers found across the Northern Hemisphere.

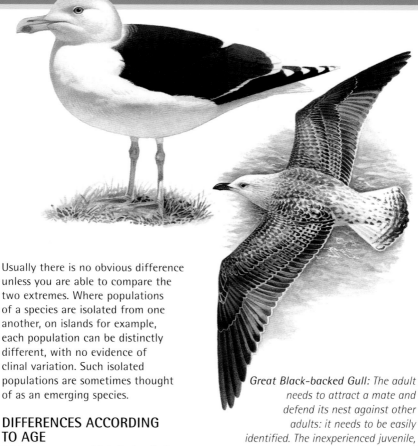

Usually there is no obvious difference unless you are able to compare the two extremes. Where populations of a species are isolated from one another, on islands for example, each population can be distinctly different, with no evidence of clinal variation. Such isolated populations are sometimes thought of as an emerging species.

Great Black-backed Gull: The adult needs to attract a mate and defend its nest against other adults: it needs to be easily identified. The inexperienced juvenile, not yet ready to mate, has no need to be identified and is better off in a dull, camouflaged color.

DIFFERENCES ACCORDING TO AGE

While most young birds look a little unlike their parents, sometimes the differences can be striking. Young gulls are mostly drab, mottled brown, and quite unlike their sharp parents. They need to stay hidden, and their brown color provides good camouflage—an adult will treat another individual in adult plumage as a potential competitor and will react aggressively toward it. It will react differently to a bird in juvenile plumage, however, recognizing that it is only a juvenile and poses no threat. Juveniles have no need to find a mate or defend their territory against intruding adults, so they do not need the bright white head, black hood, or brilliantly colored legs and bill of their parents. For several years, until they reach sexual maturity, they remain nondescript.

Typically, small songbirds rear young that are duller, browner, or more mottled than the adults in their species. Essentially, this is to help them survive their first few weeks of inexperience and ineptitude. Camouflage is vital.

DIFFERENCES ACCORDING TO SEX

Many species, including wrens, Blue Jays, Red-headed Woodpeckers, and some thrushes, have males and females that are identical. Others have marked sexual differences: Northern Cardinal, Eastern Towhee, most woodpeckers, ducks and gamebirds, such as pheasants, are good examples. In some polygamous species, such as Ruffs and Ruffed or Sage Grouse, males display together in spring so that females can choose the best mates. In Ruffs, the difference in color is heightened in spring, but in other species, such as pheasants and peacocks, the difference remains all year round. There are other instances of color difference that defy such obvious explanation. The males and females of many thrush and tyrant flycatcher species, for example, look the same. In certain species, however, such as the Eastern Bluebird (a type of thrush) and the Vermilion Flycatcher, males and females look quite different.

DIFFERENCES ACCORDING TO SEASON

Spring and summer see many male birds at their finest: they are in breeding or courtship plumage. During this time of year they need to impress females and also ward off rival males without having to fight—they can do so by looking brighter, fitter, and more dominant than their rivals.

A Black-headed Gull gains its hood in late winter; the dark hood develops from the back of the head forward so that it is complete, and most intimidating

Indian Peafowl: The gorgeous trailing plumes indicate this is a fit, experienced male. When exposed they give a good impression to the female, but it is at the price of energy expenditure and high visibility to predators.

STRUCTURAL COLOR

Some birds have feathers that glow and gleam: the electric blue of a kingfisher's back, for example, or the multiple sheens in a peacock's tail. Such color effects are too striking to be achieved by pigment alone. These strong, iridescent sheens of blue, purple, and green are produced by interference patterns that result when the structure of the feather breaks up and reflects certain wavelengths of light. A similar effect is produced by a thin film of oil lying on a pool, or by the microscopic pits on a CD tilted in a ray of sunshine.

Kingfisher: Many colorful birds rely on the structure of their feathers to separate white light and produce brilliant hues, rather like the pits on a compact disk.

to rivals, by early spring. But the hood is lost again in late summer: the molt back to white begins at the forehead and moves backward. It is as if the full extent of the hood is needed for the least possible time.

The brilliance of wildfowl males, such as goldeneyes, Mallards, and mergansers, is best seen in the winter, when the sexes pair up, often before they migrate north to breeding areas. Yet geese, which are closely related to wildfowl, have no obvious differences between male and female during the summer or winter. Similarly, wrens and Dunnocks look almost identical, regardless of the sex, age, or time of year. There is clearly no "right" way to use color and pattern, and there are many different strategies that work for different species.

CAMOUFLAGE

Birds do not have the ability to camouflage themselves as well as insects that look like leaves or fish that look like seaweed. They must be able to fly and live active lives, so they rely on their colors and patterns, rather than outlines, to help them hide. But some birds have developed wonderful camouflage: woodcocks blend in with dead leaves on the forest floor, and grouse blend into their heathery backgrounds exceedingly well. A female eider on a nest among dried seaweed or the stranded detritus of a high tide line can be nearly impossible to detect. The nightjar is also a marvelous example of a bird that can achieve near-perfect camouflage. Young birds can provide even better examples of this "cryptic" patterning: young plovers on a pebbly beach can, if they remain still, be practically invisible.

Others birds use bolder patterns to break up their outline. Adult Ring Plovers have striking areas of clear brown, black, and white that, if they stay still, make them hard to pick out against the broken background of a rocky shore.

STREAKS AND BARS

Lines of color that run more or less aligned from the front to the back of a bird are called streaks. If the marks go across from side to side, they are known as bars. A "fault bar" on a feather is a subtle, translucent bar that crosses it. These weakened areas are often caused by a varying intake of essential nutrients while the feather was growing.

Long-eared Owl

Orioles, which appear very bright in black, yellow, or orange on the page of a book, are difficult to see in the light and shade of a sunlit tree against a bright sky. Many birds the world over have darker feathers on the back than on the belly. The natural tendency for a bird's upperside to be lit by stronger light

Eurasian Woodcock: Woodcocks are among the best examples of birds with "cryptic" plumage, looking much like the litter of dead leaves on a woodland floor.

and the underside to be in shade helps "flatten out" the bird's colors and makes it more difficult to see it. Look at a thrush or robin and you will see that the flank—just where the sun tends to catch the fluffed out feathers—tends to be a little darker than the belly. This pattern of dark above and light below is known as countershading.

Such camouflage is usually a defensive mechanism that keeps the bird hidden from potential predators, but camouflage is also used as disguise by predatory birds. A sparrowhawk sitting still in the branches of a tree may not be seen by an unsuspecting bird until it is too late. A gull or tern, which has a white belly, may be hard for a fish to see against a bright sky.

Hawk Owl: The bold black face lines give owls a "fierce" look to human eyes, but they may have a different meaning in owl communications.

SHOWING OFF

Swans are so big and so strong that they really have no need for camouflage. Instead, they are dazzlingly white and brilliantly obvious to other swans from a mile away. This simple statement communicates their presence to all other birds.

White plumage is used in other ways, too. Gannets plunge from a height to catch fish, but must first spend hours flying over the sea to locate their prey. They operate in a wide, loose, extended flock: each keeps an eye on the others as well as on the sea. If one dives, the rest notice the bright white bird creating a big white splash, and they hone in on the spot, congregating rapidly above a shoal of fish.

A male pheasant uses his vivid colors and striking shape to impress a female, circling her while tilting over and spreading his feathers to the best advantage. Like the peacock with his enormous train, such birds strike a balance between the most impressive finery and practicalities: the very fact that they survive with such adornments shows how fit and experienced they must be.

Colors and patterns are used to display aggression, too. A robin spreads its red breast feathers to antagonize other robins. Usually such a show of strength and fitness is enough to avoid a fight: the bright color helps reduce the need for more drastic action. Yet, if it does not work, robins may fight to the death.

MIGRATION

The migratory patterns of birds vary enormously, even within the same species, and are related to seasonal changes in factors such as climate, the availability of food, length of day, and predation. To exploit seasonal opportunities, birds migrate vast distances in regular annual patterns.

NORTH-SOUTH DIVIDE

If there is an abundance of food anywhere on the Earth, if only for a short time, some creature will move in to exploit it. Many parts of the far north are cold and dark all winter but become, for just two or three months a year, sunlit and extremely rich in insect life during summer. To exploit this opportunity, birds must migrate south in autumn, when the food source dries up, and return north again in spring. Although most of the Northern Hemisphere's land masses lie in temperate regions where conditions are less extreme, insect-eating birds in these areas can find insects only in the warmer months and so must also move south for the winter. In North America and western Europe, many species migrate south for the winter, to South America and Africa respectively.

EAST-WEST COMPONENTS

This basic north-south pattern by no means applies to all birds that breed in the north. Many birds from Central Asia, for example, require a more easterly or westerly component in their migrations—warblers from Central Asia, for example, winter in Southeast Asia. The milder nature of winters in coastal areas compared with the severe continental weather farther inland results in many species moving southeast or southwest rather than due south in the autumn. Shorebirds breeding in northern Canada and Greenland, for example, tend to have a strong easterly component to their migration routes, exploiting the riches of the many estuaries and marshlands around the mild coasts of western Europe. Shorebirds, ducks, geese, and swans that breed in Siberia also move westward, then south around the Baltic and North Sea, to the coasts of western Europe, finding ideal refuges far to the west of their breeding ranges rather than to the south.

SOUTHERN HEMISPHERE

In the Southern Hemisphere, landmasses are smaller than in the north and mostly in or near the tropics, so bird migration is less well developed. In Australia, most movements are irregular and relate to temporary, unpredictable changes in the weather, especially droughts. In Africa, there are migrants that breed in the south and move north, but they remain within Africa south of the Sahara and their seasonal movements are not so obvious as those in Europe and North America.

However, there are dramatic exceptions among the seabirds. Great Shearwaters breed on the island group of Tristan da Cunha in the South Atlantic. Their non-breeding movements take them in a huge figure-eight around

THE HUMMINGBIRD FESTIVAL
On the south coast of Texas in the United States, migrations of hummingbirds are so striking and so predictable that each spring there are hummingbird festivals at which bird-watchers gather to see these minute migrants in favored spots. Tiny Ruby-throated Hummingbirds migrate from all over the eastern states across the Gulf of Mexico to Central America and back again, every year.

the North Atlantic, moving north in the northern summer close to North America, and swinging across to travel south again closer to the coasts of western Europe. Sooty Shearwaters from the southern Pacific have a similar vast non-breeding migration northward; and Wilson's Storm-Petrels, tiny oceanic birds that breed in the Southern Ocean, also go north beyond the Equator. However, for bigger seabirds, such as albatrosses, the area of calm seas in the tropics, known as the Doldrums, makes an effective barrier to their northward movements. They need wind to glide on and rarely cross the calmer tropics to reach northern seas.

GIGANTIC MOVEMENTS

Many millions of small songbirds, from swifts and swallows to warblers and flycatchers, migrate every year, as do hawks, owls, vultures, ducks, and even penguins. Migration times are perhaps the most exciting, unpredictable periods for bird enthusiasts, when bad weather may bring migrants to ground unexpectedly or blow them hundreds or thousands of miles off course.

There is an urgency to the move north in spring. Birds need to arrive in breeding areas as early as possible in

Vermillion Flycatchers: Hundreds of millions of tiny songbirds undertake vast migrations twice each year, often flying long distances over hostile habitats, from deserts to open oceans.

Terns: These birds are well suited to marine life, so their migrations are much less of an effort: they can feed and rest as they go.

Knots: Shorebirds such as Red Knots are among the world's greatest globetrotters, migrating from the Arctic to the southernmost tips of the continental landmasses.

order to compete for the best possible territory and to give themselves the longest possible season for rearing young. In autumn, the movement back south is much more leisurely and takes place over a longer period of time. Some species, however, make gigantic flights in single hops. Before setting off on these migrations, birds consume massive amounts of fruit and insects or other food to fuel their journey, until they are up to twice their normal weight. The tiny Ruby-throated Hummingbird often approaches such a weight gain before leaving coastal Louisiana to fly across the Gulf of Mexico to the Yucatan Peninsula.

Waders, or shorebirds, such as Hudsonian Godwits and Red Knots, must put so much energy into their northward migrations that some of their internal organs become reduced in size, processed by their bodies for energy to fuel the hugely demanding annual migrations.

DIFFERENT STRATEGIES

Those birds that breed in Arctic regions do not migrate north earlier than other species, even though they have farther to go—they actually move north late in spring or early summer, because only then will conditions in the far north be suitable. Some species have several populations that use different strategies. Some Ringed Plovers, for example, breed in the Arctic and migrate to Africa in the winter. Others breed in temperate Europe and merely migrate short distances within Europe during winter. Still others breed on coasts where the climate is mild and are able to remain there all year round. So, in spring, on the same western European beach, you may find resident Ringed Plovers that have already started to rear their chicks, winter visitors preparing to go a short distance north, and migrants from Africa passing through on their way to the Arctic. In many such species, the most northerly breeders tend to go farthest south in a kind of "leapfrog" migration. A similar leapfrog migration is seen in the American Kestrel: this species' northern-breeding populations migrate to the American tropics, and in so doing pass over more southern populations that winter in the southern United States. These northern birds also pass over other populations in Florida that reside there all year round.

Some species of shorebirds move only short distances, breeding inland on the hills and moors and simply moving to the nearest coast for the winter. Nevertheless, such movements are still regular and annual and therefore qualify as true migrations.

WANDERERS

Some species engage in sudden, irregular, or "irruptive," movements in response to overpopulation or depleted food supplies. Such movements are less predictable than typical migrations and do not include a return to the place of origin, and, therefore, they do not represent true migration.

Crossbills, for example, breed in different areas from year to year, moving to wherever there is food, which in their case is conifer seeds. Such crops are erratic, and, accordingly, so are the birds' movements. Waxwings tend to move only short distances, feeding on insects in summer and berries in winter. If the berry crop fails, however, they have

to move south and west: they "erupt" from their usual areas and "irrupt" into countries farther west and south, where flocks may appear only at intervals of several years.

SEABIRDS

Most seabirds come to land only to breed. In late summer, their busy sea-cliff colonies empty as gannets, puffins, murres, and kittiwakes fly out to sea. Puffins see out the winter storms in the mid-Atlantic. Gannets, on the other hand, do not migrate as far, except for young ones, who spend their first few years in tropical seas before returning north. It is amazing that they are able to navigate from the open, seemingly uniform oceans to the tiny islands and cliffs where they breed each spring (see Navigation, pp. 42–43).

GLOBETROTTERS

Arctic Terns probably see more daylight than any other bird. In summer they breed while immersed in near 24-hour daylight in Arctic regions. During the winter they are deep in the southern oceans, close to the Antarctic. Like the Arctic Terns, many shorebirds travel vast distances. Sanderlings, for example, breed almost as far north as any bird and can be seen in winter at the southernmost tips of Africa, Australasia, and South America. Turnstones are also long-distance travelers that breed all around the Arctic but can be seen on shorelines throughout the world outside the breeding season. These routes mean that many juvenile shorebirds have probably never seen a human before arriving on a southern coast during migration, and some people believe that this may be the reason why such birds often appear very tame.

NAVIGATION

Just how do birds find their way around the world? Experts have conducted many experiments in an attempt to unfold the mysteries of bird migration and navigation, but some remain unsolved. Bird migration remains one of the most amazing feats of animal life on Earth.

In a classic experiment, Manx Shearwaters were taken from their nests in Wales, transported across the Atlantic, and released. They found their way back within a few days. It is relatively easy to understand how a shearwater could find north or east and navigate back along the right track—if it already knew what that track should be. What is more difficult to understand is how the shearwater could possibly know which direction was home in the first place, as it was released from a dark box into an area of open ocean, with no landmarks to guide it and in a part of the world where Manx Shearwaters are not known to visit.

FINDING A WAY HOME
Pigeons that are released hundreds of miles from home circle a few times then head off in the right direction. Only when they are almost back can they find familiar landmarks.

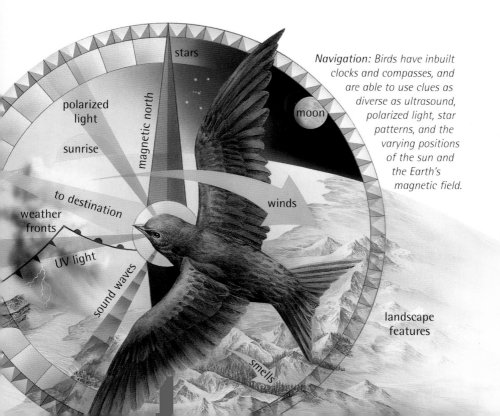

Navigation: Birds have inbuilt clocks and compasses, and are able to use clues as diverse as ultrasound, polarized light, star patterns, and the varying positions of the sun and the Earth's magnetic field.

stars

polarized light

magnetic north

moon

sunrise

to destination

winds

weather fronts

UV light

sound waves

landscape features

smells

USING THE SENSES

Intriguingly, it is likely that birds use other clues in their judgment of direction during enormous migratory flights. It is possible that smells are useful to them, and, more likely, that sounds such as ocean waves rumbling on distant shores can be detected.

If humans were moved 100 miles south and had to head north to get home, they could find the Pole Star and watch the sun rise and set and use such clues to find north. But if they were transported blindfolded and simply dropped into a forest, or put in a boat far out to sea, with no clue as to the direction taken, how could they know which way to travel to get home? This is the real mystery of bird navigation: birds have this ability.

LEARNING THE STARS

Navigation is clearly instinctive for birds: they are able to navigate without needing to calculate times and distances. Young birds growing in the nest are probably able to learn star patterns at night and can then relate these in later years to the place where they were born. This, however, only works if they have some awareness of time and season, as the relative positions of the stars are constantly moving across the sky.

Similarly, birds can use the position of the sun to fix their own position on Earth relative to where they wish to go. Some are able to ascertain the sun's position even on cloudy days, using polarized light. In another experiment, Blue-winged Teals fitted with transmitters circled up above clouds on overcast nights until they could see the stars, and then began to move in the right direction. They clearly have an internal "clock," which is essential if such astronomical information is to be of use. Pigeons that had been kept indoors in cages with lights creating artificially "out-of-phase" day lengths flew in the wrong direction when they were released, judging the sun to be in the "right" position but at the wrong time of day.

In early experiments, scientists put birds into cages inside planetariums. They arranged white filter paper around the sloping sides of the perchless cage and placed an ink pad on the small cage bottom—the only place the bird could rest. As a bird was stimulated to move according to the star patterns, so it marked its preferred direction with ink footprints on the filter paper. It was found that the birds moved in the "right" direction according to the season and the star patterns, even when these were artificially turned around.

Birds also use the Earth's magnetic field as a clue to direction. Homing pigeons, for example, have magnetic particles in the bill and the ability to use magnetic clues to navigate on days when the sun is hidden by cloud. On fine, sunny days, these magnetic influences are not needed. The sun seems to be the dominant navigating tool, but the Earth's magnetic field is a valuable backup.

SURVIVING CLIMATIC EXTREMES

A bird's efficient covering of feathers serves many functions, one of the most important of which is keeping the bird warm and dry. Nevertheless, birds are stressed by extreme weather conditions and need special adaptations to help them survive.

KEEPING COOL

Birds have no sweat glands to help them stay cool in hot weather, so they tend to stay in the shade and be most active at cooler times of the day, but further adaptations are needed. Birds such as meadowlarks or sandpipers, for example, may appear thinner in hot weather because their feathers are tightly sleeked down to squeeze out any insulating layers of air. A bird that is stressed by the heat will squat down open-mouthed and pant. Some birds, such as cormorants and gannets, pulsate the fleshy pouch under the chin to lose excess heat through the evaporation of water from the mouth lining. New World Vultures and storks cool off by excreting on their legs, so that moisture can evaporate from the excrement.

During hot weather, nesting birds may stand over their eggs, using their shadows to keep the eggs cool. In North America, Southern Killdeer soak their

STUCK IN THE MIDDLE

Starlings and cowbirds roost in dense flocks. This is not just for protection from predators, but because the older, more experienced birds can find warm spots in the center, while younger, weaker, less dominant ones take their chance on the cooler fringes of the flock.

belly feathers in nearby pools then drip water onto their eggs to cool them. The desert-dwelling sandgrouse transports water from distant pools in its belly feathers to cool its eggs or to give its chicks a vital drink. In cold weather, however, these same birds fluff out their feathers, and formerly slender birds then look dumpy and rotund.

KEEPING WARM

A bird's body feathers extend over the tops of the legs, which are kept warm by the insulating layers of feathers and the air trapped between the feathers and the skin. To reduce heat loss from bare surfaces, a bird may stand on one leg

Rock Ptarmigan: Birds that live at high-altitudes, like the Rock Ptarmigan, and in the far north are specifically adapted to their fiercely cold habitat, and climate change spells a gloomy future for them.

for long periods, with the other tucked away. A bird may also tuck its bill back inside its shoulder feathers, where it can breathe in warmer air trapped between the feathers and the skin.

Birds that live in the far north tend to be bigger than their close relatives or similar species farther south. Larger birds have a smaller surface area per unit of volume and so lose less heat via radiation when cold. Birds have adapted to cold climates in other ways, too: Rock Ptarmigans, which live in the Arctic and high on exposed mountaintops, have densely-feathered feet.

Small birds eat more when it's cold, some consuming almost their own weight in food each day to get enough energy to survive the long nights.

In winter, there are fewer daylight feeding hours and more hours of cold darkness to survive and birds find sheltered, warm places in which to roost. Some, such as Pied Wagtails in Europe, roost in flocks in ornamental trees in town squares, or in the roofs of greenhouses, railway stations, or factories. Such places will be much warmer than the open countryside. Birds such as chickadees abandon their normal practice of individual roosts and roost close together, so that they share body heat and warm the air around them.

Dowitcher: This dowitcher has one leg tucked away to keep warm. Like other wetland species with long, sensitive bills, it moves away in a hard frost to find soft ground where it can probe for food.

Chickadees can even reduce their body temperature by several degrees at night, in order to reduce their metabolic rates and conserve energy.

Young swifts can also reduce their temperature and go into torpor—a kind of mini-hibernation—on dull, cold days, when their parents find it difficult to provide sufficient food.

PREENING TO SURVIVE
A bird's plumage needs to be smooth, clean, and waterproof if it is to have a good chance of survival. To keep the feathers in good condition, birds preen daily, removing parasites and smearing oil over the feathers to keep them waterproof. The structure of the feather allows it to "breathe" while being waterproof, provided it is kept in good condition.

GENERATING ENERGY
Hummingbirds are tiny but incredibly active and energetic, with one of the highest metabolic rates of any animal. Their rate of energy use and conversion of food and oxygen into energy is about 12 times that of a pigeon—but to maintain this, hummingbirds must consume their own weight in nectar daily. Most cannot manage this in winter in North America and they therefore migrate south: Anna's Hummingbird can survive all year in California.

FOOD AND FEEDING

The great diversity of birds is largely due to the many different kinds of food that they can exploit, along with the variety of their habitats and the isolation of species by geographic barriers. Most species of birds are adapted to feed on something very slightly different from their close neighbors, so that competition for prey is kept low.

In general, birds eat feverishly early in the morning after having fasted all night. Then they rest, feed casually during the day, then feed feverishly again before going to roost for the night.

FOOD FROM THE TREES
Brown Creepers feed on minute insects and spiders, including their eggs and larvae, on the bark of trees. They explore the tiniest crevices using their thin, curved bills. Nuthatches also explore the bark but are more likely to take larger food and eat far more seeds and berries. They have stronger feet for a better grip, which makes them more agile, and bigger bills to tackle larger food items—they can even hammer open tough nuts.

Chickadees and titmice also explore tree bark and foliage. The Tufted Titmouse tends to prefer the bark of the trunks and bigger branches of trees,

Common Snipe: The bill is flexible but strong enough to open underground and grasp a worm.

as well as finding food on the ground below, while smaller chickadees feed on slimmer branches and twigs, looking for smaller prey. In this way, these different species can move together as a flock, keeping their eyes open for possible danger, while keeping out of each other's way and eating different food.

Chickadees find an abundance of food at different times of the year and hide a lot of it by pushing it into places that they are likely to search again later, such as bunches of pine needles. These stores of food can then be saved for the winter. While chickadees find stored food again by chance, various crows, jays, and magpies locate their stored food by design. They bury nuts, scraps of meat, and acorns and can remember where they put their winter stores months later.

BENEATH THE SURFACE
Shorebirds feed in rhythm with the tides, so their feeding times fluctuate from day to day, always coming at low tide. Wading birds on a beach use different feeding strategies too. A Semipalmated (with toes webbed for part of their length) Plover picks small shellfish and crustaceans from the surface of the mud, while a Semipalmated Sandpiper or a Dunlin picks from an abundance of minute snails barely hidden in the

wet mud at low tide. A Red Knot has a longer bill and probes a little more deeply. Godwits probe deeper still for small worms, while curlews, which have very long bills, probe deep down for bigger lugworms, as well as taking ragworms, shellfish, and small crabs from rock pools as the tide falls. Each in its own way is adapted to feed on different food, or in different situations, so that all can live together on the same beach.

Flycatcher: While warblers mostly have fine, thin bills, flycatchers have broader bills with bristles around them, making it easier to snap-up flying insects.

CLIMATE CHANGE

Many seed-eating birds, such as finches and sparrows, need to eat insects during the summer. The adult birds manage to survive on only seeds, but their fast-growing chicks must have energy-rich, high-protein food, and the best source is insect food. Finches feed thousands of leaf-eating caterpillars to their young in the nest. Recently, tits have had poorer breeding seasons, and this may be because they are nesting at the "usual" time, while their caterpillar food is emerging two or three weeks earlier due to the effects of climate change. Global warming is wreaking havoc in some places as the reproductive cycles of birds and their prey are becoming out of sync.

NO CONTEST

A remarkable means of avoiding competition is seen in birds of prey, especially in bird-eating hawks, such as Cooper's and Sharp-shinned Hawks—the female is up to one-third bigger than the male. This means that the sexes eat prey of different sizes and so do not compete with one another, allowing them to survive together in a smaller area without straining the supply of food.

HOW TO FEED BIRDS
IN THE GARDEN

Feeding garden birds has become a multi-million dollar business. The trend began in North America and followed later on in Europe. Today, the new foods that are being used in bird feeders are attracting different kinds of birds, and present the food in ever more sophisticated ways.

Bird lovers feed garden birds for two main reasons: to help birds survive in a tougher environment, and to see them up close. Fortunately, the two are mutually beneficial.

POSITIONING A FEEDER
To get a good view of birds feeding in your garden, the feeder must be placed so that you can see it from a normal position within the house. A feeding tray must be high enough that you can easily see it while sitting down in a favorite comfortable chair. It is no use if it is hidden below the window level.

The feeder should be placed away from any cold, windy channel between walls or buildings—a little shelter is always welcome. It is also a good idea to position it away from a footpath, where the birds may be disturbed.

Any feeder is vulnerable to predation: if you put out foods to attract birds, you will attract hawks and other predators, too. A bird feeder covered in tits provides an easy meal for a hawk. There is no way to eliminate this danger, but you can do things to minimize the risk. The most effective solution is a dome of large-mesh chicken wire placed over the feeder, which will allow smaller birds to enter while keeping predators out. Netting is likely to be chewed through by squirrels. Suspending unwanted CDs from loose strings on the feeder may distract both hawks and the songbirds you want to attract—but this deterrent will not last.

If you place a feeder close to a bush or tree, it gives small birds a sporting chance of diving to safety. On the other hand, positioning a feeder by thick shrubbery or a flowerbed might invite unwanted attention from the local cat, the garden bird's greatest enemy.

WHEN TO FEED BIRDS
You can feed birds all year round. Birds need food in winter to help them survive the cold nights, but spring can also be a

DIFFERENT TECHNIQUES
Try putting fat and cheese in crevices in tree bark, and scatter grated cheese under bushes for shy birds that don't come to tables. Feeding birds in several places will attract a greater number and variety, and allow birds to feed without constantly squabbling.

difficult time for them. Those that rely on seeds and fruit can find that natural supplies are at their lowest ebb by late spring and a free handout of birdseeds and peanuts can be a real boost just before the breeding season.

Remember that young birds are being fed in the nest during spring and summer. Although most birds will not feed their chicks food that might endanger them, if natural food is scarce, they may resort to feeding them foods such as peanuts. Baby birds can choke on large peanuts, so make sure they are crushed and crumbled, or wrap them in a strong mesh that is fine enough to make birds peck pieces from them, rather than take them away whole.

TYPES OF FEEDERS

Do not use flexible feeders. One neat design is the coil spring feeder with a base and lid—but make sure the coil is very rigid. A flexible coil may catch the legs and feet of feeding birds and injure or kill them. Peanuts have long been sold in plastic mesh bags, which can be hung outside as ready-made feeders. These are generally fine to use, but increasingly people have become aware that they can trap and kill small birds. Birds can get their feet and even their tongue tangled in the mesh so that they hang from it until they die. It is best to avoid such bags and instead place the nuts inside a rigid metal mesh basket or a plastic tube with special feeding ports.

Feeder types: Rigid spiral metal feeders (above left) are safe, but springy ones may trap birds' feet. Solid-mesh feeders (above center) are ideal for bulky foods; special tubes (above right) are needed for finer seeds.

FOODS TO OFFER BIRDS

Feeding birds in a garden can be great fun: you can experiment with different foods and the way you offer them. There are types of bird foods available to suit every budget, from expensive seeds to cheap kitchen scraps. Just remember to keep everything clean. Piles of old bird droppings or decaying food can promote disease and wipe out the very birds you are trying to save.

Plant shrubs and herbs—especially species native to your area—in the garden to help birds find food. Many of these plants provide nectar and attract insects, which birds eat. Others produce fruits—all kinds of berry-bearing shrubs are excellent for birds, especially cotoneasters, berberis, and hawthorns, as well as pyracantha and holly. Such natural foods are good for birds and keep a natural balance in the garden.

If you have feeders and a birdtable, or a ground feeder, you can do a great deal to help birds. They need energy, which often means fat: full-fat cheese, cooked bacon rind, suet, and animal fats make perfect foods and can also form the basis of "bird cakes."

To make a bird cake, use the fatty material to bind together nuts, seeds, fruits, and scraps. Squeeze or pour the mixture into containers such as yogurt pots and coconut shells. Hung in trees or from the birdtable, these are great feeders that offer food for winter birds. Do not put such fat-based foods out in the summer heat. The fat melts and can cause feather damage and loss as the oils soak into the bird's plumage.

THE RIGHT FOODS

Bread is a good type of food to provide birds in small quantities. Brown, damp bread is preferable—dry, crusty bread is often neglected. Stale cake crumbled on the birdtable or on the ground is often a better choice. Kitchen scraps of all kinds, from uncooked or cooked pastry to bits of fruit, will usually be accepted.

Apples also make good food, especially if they are cut into small pieces or halved and scattered on the ground for thrushes, or put on the birdtable. Scatter them in several places if you have space, so that a number of birds can feed without fighting.

Peanuts are a popular, traditional food for birds and remain ideal, especially for tits when hung in a mesh or special tubular feeder—but many finches and other birds will eat them, too. Woodpeckers often find them and come frequently to feed on them.

Sunflower seeds are excellent, oily food for birds such as the larger finches, and are a great alternative to peanuts. Smaller finches will also eat oats and millet scattered on the ground or a table or placed in a feeder. Nyjer, or niger, seed is a much finer seed that requires special feeders. It may not work, but when it does, it can attract goldfinches and siskins and keep dozens of them coming back for weeks. It is, however, quite expensive.

Wild bird seeds come in many mixtures, from cheap seeds to pricey high-protein mixes. Cheaper seeds have

FEEDING TIPS

When you feed the birds, take the following steps to provide a safe and healthy feeding environment.

• Position feeding stations in different areas of your yard to spread birds around and avoid competition, stress, and disease.

• Clean your feeders regularly with hot water, and let them dry completely. Keep areas under and around the feeders clean.

• Keep seed clean and dry and watch that it doesn't get moldy. If there is a lot of waste, reduce the amount of food you put out.

• Use a seed blend that is designed for the feeder you have and the type of birds that come to that feeder.

• Offer seeds in a feeder rather than scattering seed on the ground.

• If possible, move your feeding stations periodically, so there will be less concentration of bird droppings.

• Always wash your hands after filling or cleaning your feeders.

• Place bird feeders in locations that do not provide hiding places where cats and other predators can wait to ambush the feeder. Bird feeders should be placed 5–12 inches (12.5–30 cm) from low shrubs or bushes that provide cover.

• Place the feeder 5–12 feet (1.5–3.5 m) from a brush pile or bushes to provide a place for birds to take cover in the event of danger.

a lot of large grains, which are not eaten by many birds other than pigeons, and may even be padded out for bulk with substances such as broken dog biscuit. Try to choose better quality foods from reputable sources.

Don't feed birds salted foods, such as salted peanuts, potato chips, or salty bacon. Also avoid giving desiccated coconut and other dried foods that may swell after they are swallowed.

WATER

Fresh water is vital for birds, all year round: even in the depths of winter they need to drink and they need to bathe. Put out a dish or fill a birdbath each day. Keep the water clean, and never use any artificial substances to prevent the water from freezing.

HYGIENE

Cleanliness is important for birds and every bit as vital for you. Use rubber gloves when handling feeders and cleaning tables; use a stiff brush and keep it solely for the purpose of cleaning your birdtable. Move your feeders around every so often to avoid a buildup of droppings and waste. Now and then, wash them in a weak solution of ordinary bleach and rinse them clean.

A territory is an area that one bird, or a pair, defends from other birds of the same species—or sometimes a different species—so that it can use nesting sites and roosting places in the area and have access to food without interference or competition, whereas in colonies, birds generally stay together.

Most species have breeding territories but, for the rest of the year, some species can be found in flocks, although each individual usually defends a small personal space as it feeds. Some, such as shelducks, have territories to nest in, but also another territory nearby, in which their young grow up. Many others have winter feeding territories.

SEASONAL TERRITORIES

Both summer and winter territories help to regulate bird numbers to a level that the habitat can support. Species such as goldfinches feed on seeds that are locally abundant; they have very small nesting territories and do not have winter territories, other than a small personal space that they defend as they move—there is enough food for many to feed together. But chaffinches and blue tits need a supply of caterpillars to feed their chicks in the spring. As caterpillars are widely but more thinly spread, they must defend exclusive feeding territories to ensure a steady supply.

Feeding territories are important for most birds, even in winter. Waders feed on mudflats at low tide, but together at high tide. Some, such as the larger plovers, defend feeding territories at

Safety in numbers: Concentrations of breeding birds benefit from many pairs of eyes looking out for danger.

low tide and battle for those with the most food. Those with the best spots are likely to be fitter by the spring, ready for migration, ready to find a breeding territory in the Arctic, and are brighter and more likely to attract a mate. The poorly nourished ones will be weaker, duller, and less successful.

Kingfishers need a territory along a river or stream. The competition is so great that a pair of kingfishers must drive their offspring away within a few weeks of their fledging as there will not be enough fish to feed the whole family for long. In autumn, young kingfishers have to find territories of their own and are more likely to die at this time than any other. "Survival of the fittest" seems to be the rule.

Pied Flycatchers set up feeding territories in Spain, while they are on migration between Africa and northern Europe, to get fitter for the breeding season ahead.

COLONIES

It may seem that colonies are the opposite of breeding territories, as birds squeeze together to nest. Pairs, however, usually keep at least a certain distance apart—in gannets and terns, it is the length of a vicious peck at the neighbors. Guillemots, however, nest in limited space on narrow ledges and rub shoulder to shoulder. Rooks breed in treetop colonies, but spend a lot of time trying to steal nest material from each other and defending their own nest.

For these birds, breeding in colonies allows some group defense against predators and also provides opportunity for the transfer of information about good feeding sites. They do not need a large territory because they fly off to feed at sea, or out on farmland, far from the colony, and manage to find most of their food elsewhere.

Closed world: Gannets have such rigidly defined social interactions that only when the colony reaches a certain size does their breeding really take off.

SONG, COURTSHIP, AND DISPLAY

During the spring, a territorial bird (usually a male, but sometimes a female or a pair) has to find a territory that will support himself, a mate, and their young. Birds use song to attract a mate, repel rivals, or both. Courtship involves ritualized displays that help break down a bird's instinct to maintain individual distance and strengthen a pair bond. Such displays often have different meanings from species to species.

Lapwing: This shorebird combines striking colors and shapes, distinctive calls, and a wild, tumbling flight in its displays.

By singing, a male bird tells other males that an area is occupied—it is a clear message that provides birds with space that is free of competition and interference—and the space usually comes as a result of song rather than potentially injurious physical conflict.

SONG

Songs are specific to each species. Basic songs, such as a wren's, are simple and have little variation. Longer, more sophisticated songs develop with age as the bird adds to its repertoire, to show how mature and experienced it is. A rich variety of songs is used by the Marsh Warbler in the U.K. and the Northern Mockingbird in North America, which add to their repertoire by imitating a vast range of other birds—maybe 100 or more. The Marsh Warbler even includes mimicry of birds it encounters in its winter in Africa. The reason for this behavior is unknown—in males, it may be simply a method of displaying virtuosity to the females. At the other end of the scale, a young bird deprived of hearing others of its species will grow up using an ordinary, simple, "low-quality" version of its species song, reflecting the song's inherited nature but also the influence of competition with and imitation of others. If two birds that have not yet claimed a territory both want to settle in the same area, and both have a more or less equal interest in and access to it, they may fight ferociously. Male birds generally fight other males, and females fight other females—sometimes, but rarely, to the death. If two males are both settled in their own territories and meet at the boundary between them, they will call, sing, and display to avoid fighting. If one bird trespasses, the other, defending, bird will usually manage to drive it away.

COURTSHIP

In many songbirds, and some other birds such as terns, the male feeds the female during courtship and early in the breeding season. Such courtship feeding aids in pair bonding, but also helps the female survive a period of stress, when she is using huge amounts of energy to lay a large clutch of eggs.

DISPLAY

In large birds of prey, such as larger hawks and eagles, aerial displays take the place of song. Sounds do not carry far in the huge territories of these birds, but they can see each other from great distances. These birds spend hours soaring over their nesting areas so that others of their species can see, and keep away.

Not all birds form long-lasting pair bonds when breeding. Game birds such as grouse and pheasants are polygynous, meaning that one male mates with two or more females; the males fight and show off but it is the females that select a mate. Such fights and displays are highly ritualized, and often take place at traditional sites that have been used for decades. Black Grouse in Europe and Greater Prairie Chickens in North America, for example, collect in spring at a place called a "lek." The males strut, spread their tails, jump in the air, make special sounds, and occasionally fight. The females look on, deciding which is the "best" male to father their young.

Wild Turkey: A big, healthy turkey is an impressive sight even to us. Its performance must impress both rivals and potential mates.

Bird calls have different functions from song. Song is used, primarily by male birds, to warn other males to keep away or to attract females. Females of some species, such as the Northern Cardinal in North America, sometimes sing to defend a territory against other females, but their song is more muted than that of males. Calls, on the other hand, are used by birds of all ages and both sexes.

Some calls are simply used to keep in touch, while others give particular messages, even to birds of other species. Certain postures and actions function in a similar way.

CONTACT CALLS

A flock of small birds moving through the woods during the winter keeps more or less together in order to maintain vigilance against predators and to improve the chances that one member of the flock will find food that all can exploit. Birds within the flock keep in touch by rather quiet, simple, short call notes, called contact calls.

Moorhens: The splash of white beneath the tail is used as a means of communication between mates and also between rivals.

Such calls often have a long vowel sound but, to our ears, no obvious consonants—they do not have "hard" endings or "shapes" to the sound, and they can often be written down as "eeee" or "sseee." Similar notes, but with a greater intensity and a sharp or metallic quality, give warning of a predator. These calls are often above the frequency range that is easily heard by a large hawk or falcon, but well within the hearing of small songbirds.

IDENTIFYING CALLS

The lack of a hard edge to call notes also makes them exceedingly difficult to locate. Bird-watchers often hear calls but find it hard to locate the bird that is making the sounds. This allows a small bird to warn others that a predator is near without putting itself at risk. House sparrows use different calls to indicate

aerial threats and ground-based threats, such as a cat. If you become familiar with the alarm notes of different birds, you may find that you can recognize the call a bird makes to identify the presence of a hawk, and may improve your chances of seeing these birds of prey.

Acting up: A "broken wing" display is designed to lure predators in pursuit of easy prey away from eggs or chicks.

WARNING CALLS

Adult birds use particular warning calls for their chicks, too. "Keep still" is the obvious meaning of a call when danger approaches. Young birds make long, loud, whining, or squealing notes when they are hungry. One theory to explain such behavior is that it "blackmails" the parents into feeding their chicks to keep them quiet, otherwise, the sounds would attract predators and weeks of effort spent rearing the young would be wasted. An extreme example of this is the young cuckoo, which is reared by foster parents and has a kind of "super" food-begging call. It is so effective that even passing birds that have nothing to do with the cuckoo will stop to feed it. Its loud, wheezing, begging note seems to be an irresistible stimulus.

Small birds make loud alarm calls when they discover a predator, such as an owl roosting in a tree by day. They risk great danger in drawing attention

to the owl by "mobbing" it, bringing in a crowd of birds of several species that join in the hue and cry. This may be to make sure that all birds in the area know that the owl is there, or it may help to drive the owl away, or it may even teach young birds that owls are dangerous. Another theory is that such a noise attracts even bigger creatures—such as people—that scare the owl away when they come to investigate.

POSTURES

A good example of a posture is the injury-feigning of birds such as plovers and skuas. If a predator such as a cat or fox threatens the nest or young, the parent will flutter along the ground, luring the predator away by pretending to be injured and unable to fly. The potential predator misses a meal when the adult judges its young to be safe, suddenly "recovers" and flies away.

NESTS

The main purpose of any bird is to reproduce and ensure the survival of its species: to do so, it must find a mate, and females must nest, lay eggs, and see that their chicks are reared. A nest is simply a receptacle—or even a mere scrape in the ground—in which the eggs are laid and incubated until they hatch.

In many species the young remain in the nest until they can fly. Once the nest has fulfilled its purpose—by which time it may be an unsavory and unhygienic place containing various parasites, droppings, and uneaten scraps of food—it is usually neglected. Some larger species, however, build more substantial nests, which are refurbished year after year—the nests built by eagles and Ospreys may become very large.

Earth nest: Terns, gulls, and wading birds lay their eggs in a scraped hollow in earth or sand.

NEST USES

A nest is the place where a bird lays its eggs and incubates them until they hatch. It is not a "home" used by birds at other times, although some hole nests are used as roosting sites

Eagle nest: Many big birds of prey reuse big stick nests, which can become enormous over many years.

in winter. A nest or nest site may be used many times over, or a new one may be made for each set of eggs. In general, small birds use new nests for each clutch during a season, as the nest becomes a dirty and unhygienic place after rearing a family: it tends to harbor many parasites, such as mites, ticks, and fleas, probably has waste food in and around it, and is soiled with droppings. Larger birds, which have just one clutch each year, are more likely to reuse a nest in successive seasons, provided at least one of the pair survives: in some species, such as Ospreys and Golden Eagles, nests may be used by generations of birds over decades, and others, such as Peregrine Falcons and ravens, use the same piece of cliff, if not the same ledge, for many years.

BIRDS WITH NO NEST

Not all species build a structure for the nest: some simply lay eggs directly onto the bare ground, onto a cliff ledge, or inside a hole, without any nest material being added. Kingfishers lay onto a bare floor inside a deep tunnel, but as the eggs hatch and the young grow, their nest chamber fills with bits of fish and undigested fish bones, as well as foul, semi-liquid droppings.

Some birds such as guillemots and other seabirds, and Peregrine Falcons, lay eggs on a bare ledge, or at best a scrape in earth or gravel naturally collected on a cliff ledge. Hygiene here is also suspect: seabirds in colonies may be splashed with droppings from birds on ledges higher up the cliff. Birds of prey, however, while they may build up unwanted food that simply rots around the nest, usually at least keep the nest free from droppings, and the young birds quickly learn to back up to the side of the nest and void their excreta over the edge. Other birds, such as plovers, add a few scraps of vegetation, shells, or stones to a scrape on the ground or in a sandy beach and the addition of such objects can become ritualized.

Woodpecker nest: Even firm, healthy wood can be chipped away by a woodpecker as it excavates its round, deep nesting hole.

Ledge nest: Some birds of prey, including Peregrine Falcons, nest on earthy ledges on the face of cliffs.

NEST MATERIALS

While falcons make no nest, hawks do so, usually in trees. Eagles and Ospreys can build up huge nests using sticks, which accumulate over decades of repeated use, creating incredible structures on cliffs, poles, or in treetops. They also bring green foliage to the nest all summer, perhaps to help keep down flies and pests in a nest full of rotting food.

In those birds that do build nests, often both sexes share the work, but the female may add the final lining. In many cases the male makes the initial foundations. Male wrens make several nests as part of their courtship routine: they attract females and show them a choice of nests, perching nearby and waving their wings as they encourage the female to inspect each site, but the female makes the final choice of which one to use.

Many nests are simple structures of sticks and twigs, usually with a lining of smaller materials and perhaps feathers, hair, or fine plant fibers. Such a nest made by a small songbird can be completed within two days: other more complex structures may take a week or two to complete. Magpies add a protective dome to their "fortress" nests. Small songbirds make more complex structures, usually cup-shaped, with a softer lining; those of the thrushes, such as American Robins and the European Blackbird, have a strong, hard mud layer inside a basic structure of grasses and twigs. Some, such as the Long-tailed Tit's nest, or the smaller, hammock-like nests of Goldcrests and kinglets, are beautiful, delicate, and made of lichens and moss held together with spider's webs. These nests stretch as the brood of chicks grows. Wildfowl pluck down from their own bodies to add a warm, soft layer to the inside of the nest.

HOLE NESTS

Many birds nest in holes of some kind: woodpeckers chip out a hole in a tree, while kingfishers dig into an earth bank. Birds as varied as chickadees and tits, owls, and kestrels occupy a hole in a tree—either a natural hole or one made by a woodpecker. Nuthatches of several species plaster up the entrance hole with mud, until it is just big enough to allow them in, but excludes larger predators. They will also plaster mud between a nest box and the bole of a tree, which perhaps insulates the box and provides greater stability. The plastering habit is probably simply instinctive and used whether it has a necessary function or not: nuthatches cannot resist doing it.

Songbird nest: A typical small bird's nest is a cup-shaped structure, often with a softer lining.

ARTIFICIAL NESTS

Birds that nest in holes can be helped, even in gardens, by the use of artificial nest boxes. In the U.K., Blue and Great Tits are common nest box occupants, while populations of Pied Flycatchers have been increased in many woodlands by the provision of boxes where natural holes are few. In the U.S.A., Purple Martins will use large "apartment house" boxes on special poles, and bluebirds can be helped by the provision of boxes in and around gardens. Special boxes can be used by owls and kestrels, while artificial structures that provide shelter for chicks have helped rare birds such as Roseate Terns improve their breeding success on nature reserves, where severe weather and predators otherwise take their toll.

NEST BOXES

Nest boxes can easily be made to standard sizes and designs from wood, or "woodcrete"—a mixture of sawdust and cement—which helps to protect eggs and chicks from the attentions of woodpeckers and other predators that can gain access to a normal wooden box. While metal shields around the entrance may deter some predators, woodpeckers can still dig their way in from the side unless a more resilient material is used.

Nest box: These structures can be made in many shapes and sizes according to the bird you have in mind: this one would suit a small hole-nester.

Tenement blocks: The Purple Martin has been exclusively nesting in this style of nest box for nearly a century in the eastern part of North America.

EGGS

Birds lay eggs and incubate them externally, in nearly all cases by applying heat from their bodies, until the young bird breaks free. Some small songbird eggs hatch in fewer than 10 days, but the eggs of some species, particularly many seabirds, may require 50 days or more. Albatross eggs, for example, take as long as 80 days to hatch.

Bird eggs contain a developing embryo and various components that nourish and protect it—the yolk, egg white (or albumen), and an air cell. These elements are encased in a more or less smooth, thin, rigid calcium shell of surprising strength that keeps out water, but allows in air. Eggs may be almost round, symmetrically oval or, most often, broader at one end than the other. The narrow end of an egg may be blunt or rather pointed, as in the case of some ground-nesting birds like the Killdeer in North America, which lay four eggs and arrange them neatly, with the pointed ends directed inwards.

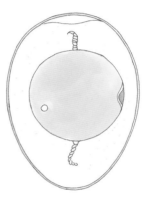

Parts of an egg: The egg yolk is held in place within the white, or albumen; at the broad end of the egg is an air cell.

EGG DESIGN

As the egg is formed, colors and patterns that are characteristic of the species may be laid down on the shell. These sometimes help to camouflage the egg when it is left uncovered in the nest. Hole-nesting birds, including owls and woodpeckers, lay white eggs, which are more easily seen in poor light.

The patterns of an egg are not simply a superficial coloring on the outside of the egg: some markings, such as dark spots and blotches, often concentrated towards the broader end of the egg, are integral parts of the shell's structure. The extra pigment in these blotches strengthens weak areas in the thinnest parts of the shell and they may have other functions as yet unknown.

Eggs are incubated by one or both parents. An adult bird sits on the eggs to warm them until they hatch, usually with the aid of an "incubation patch"— bare skin on the belly of the incubating bird with no feathers but expanded blood vessels to supply extra heat. The developing chick receives nutrients from the yolk inside the egg and eventually breaks through the shell, using a tiny "tooth" at the tip of its bill.

Chicks can be described as either nidicolous (altricial) or nidifugous

Nidicolous chick: Many chicks hatch out tiny, blind, and naked and then develop within the nest for several days.

Nidifugous chick: Some chicks hatch with a downy coat, strong legs, and good vision and leave the nest within hours.

(precocial). Nidicolous chicks are weak, more or less naked, and blind, and they remain in the nest, needing care and shelter until they grow a covering of feathers and are ready to fly. Nidifugous chicks are covered in warm down, are bright-eyed and active, leave the nest within a matter of hours, and immediately find their own food.

Most songbirds are nidicolous, while most terns, sandpipers, plovers, and chicken-like birds are nidifugous. Many species have chicks that are somewhat intermediate to these. The nestlings of hawks, owls, and herons, for example,

are downy and more developed at hatching than those of most songbirds. They are somewhat active when hatched and soon move about onto branches of their nest tree. Some, such as gull chicks, leave the nest in a downy covering, but require more care and feeding than typical nidifugous chicks.

All chicks need to be cared for to some extent, and they are brooded by a parent when they are cold and wet—the brooding adult typically calls the chicks, which nestle among the adult breast and belly feathers or under a drooped wing for warmth and protection.

HOW MANY EGGS?
A full set of eggs is called a clutch. Some long-lived birds that have a long period of immaturity, such as fulmars, lay a single egg each year. Small songbirds may lay one clutch of 10 to 12 eggs, their hatching coinciding with the peak availability of suitable food. Others produce two, three, or even four clutches of 3 to 5 eggs each during a season. Gamebirds, such as quail and pheasants, have only one clutch each year, but may lay up to 15 eggs; sometimes eggs are laid in the same nest by more than one female.

REARING A FAMILY

Having put so much effort into finding and defending a territory, finding a mate, building a nest, and producing eggs, a parent bird must ensure that its young survive and thrive. To do so, it must defend them from predators, shelter them from hot sun, cold wind, or rain, and keep them well fed.

Chicks on the ground, such as those of plovers, seem extremely vulnerable, but they can scatter when danger threatens. Plover chicks also have excellent camouflage and quickly learn to "freeze," crouching stock still until a parent calls to say that danger has passed. In many ways, songbird chicks in a nest are more vulnerable. The nest may be well hidden and provide shelter, but the chicks are unable to move. Once they are found, there is no escape.

DEFENDING THE YOUNG

Even small birds fight against hawks, cats, and foxes as best they can. Birds as diverse as swallows, mockingbirds, terns, hawks, and owls may dive at the head of a person who comes too close to a nest containing chicks. Other birds, such as many sparrows, discreetly leave their nest when danger threatens: it is better for the parent to survive than to stay to face a human intruder and risk death, and the nest is less likely to be found if the parent bird is absent.

Even doves, particularly unsuited to aggressive attacks, have been seen diving at a small hawk that has caught a chick. Skuas are much more dynamic, aggressive birds, and they will dive at the head of a person near their breeding area, sometimes striking them. Female harriers, and much smaller Arctic Terns, practice similar behavior.

FEEDING THE FAMILY

Small birds such as tits visit the nest hundreds of times each day to bring food for a growing family. Chicks require a constant supply of energy and need brooding in bad weather—the parent shelters them under its wings and fluffed-out body feathers. Swifts feed their young on flying insects—not as reliable a food source as caterpillars and insects found on foliage. If the weather is wet and windy, the swifts may find it difficult to find food. At such times their chicks become temporarily torpid (they lower their body temperature and become inactive, thus conserving energy)—but swifts may fly hundreds of miles to avoid bad weather, or to exploit insects concentrated along weather fronts. They are among the finest meteorologists in the bird world.

In several species—as varied as Common Moorhens, Long-tailed Tits, Florida Scrub Jays, and Red-cockaded Woodpeckers—parent birds receive help to feed their young from other birds. In Common Moorhens, the young from an early brood help to feed chicks of a later brood. In Long-tailed Tits, helpers are usually brothers of the male parent, with no chicks of their own. In Florida Scrub Jays and Red-cockaded Woodpeckers, the helpers are usually offspring from previous years.

ENVIRONMENTAL EFFECTS

Some seabirds have struggled in recent years to find food for their chicks. Rising sea temperatures have affected the distribution and abundance of plankton, which are eaten by sand eels, the favored prey of some seabirds. Kittiwakes, terns, and guillemots have been seen catching dozens of tough, leathery pipefish, which have replaced the sand eels in some areas, and trying to feed them to their chicks. The chicks starve, surrounded by uneaten fish, which they are unable to swallow—many choke to death in the attempt. Global warming is also affecting the migratory patterns of some songbirds, which are returning earlier to their breeding grounds. In some cases, the young of these birds are hatching before the insects the parents need to gather for them are emerging, with catastrophic results. Nesting efforts fail for lack of food, and when subsequent insect emergence peaks, it remains uncontrolled by the lowered bird population.

Feeding chicks: Tiny chicks call loudly as long as they are hungry. This forces the parents to either keep feeding them or risk losing the results of weeks of intensive effort.

MAKING THE MOST OF BIRDING

This chapter contains expert tips, techniques, and advice on how best to observe birds: where, when, and what to look for, basic identification, taking notes, making sketches, or taking photographs. This section also deals with how birds are coping in our fast-changing, increasingly urbanized world: what does intensive farming mean for native habitats? Is ecotourism a good thing? How do the suspected effects of climate change upset the natural balance?

TELLING BIRDS APART

Each species of bird is identifiably different in some way from other bird species. In many cases, the differences are obvious, but in others they are less so and may come down to extremely subtle variations in color, shape, or even the sounds a bird makes. The difficulty of identifying birds therefore varies from easy-for-beginners to challenging—even for specialists.

Beginners to bird-watching should start by identifying common garden and town birds. It is a good idea to get a few basic reference points—the commonest, simplest species—against which other birds can be compared. When you observe a "new" bird you can then think about how it looks compared with the birds you already know. Is it about the size of a sparrow, or as big as a pigeon? Is it the same shape as a robin, or similar to a starling but with a thicker bill? Such basic comparisons are invaluable and your bank of references will grow as you get to know more and more birds. You will then be able to make far more subtle and useful comparisons.

NOTING SIZE, SHAPE, AND BEHAVIOR

The size of a bird is one of the first points you should note. This is not always easy, unless the bird is near another species or object with which you are familiar. It can be hard to judge the size of a bird that is flying high in the sky or perched far away across a

GO PISH

There are several ways in which you can lure small songbirds to come closer so you can get a better look. "Pishing"—making a repeated, urgent "pshhh pshhh" sound—is one such method. This noise imitates that of a worried bird. Squeaking, with high-pitched squealing and squeaking sounds, also works well. You can also try playing the calls or songs of a bird on a CD to force a particular bird to approach to defend his territory against an intruder. This technique can work like magic, but it should be used sparingly and with caution. It tends to be disruptive and can be damaging for the bird. Use the playback technique with great restraint or not at all. Finally, some refuges and sanctuaries forbid the use of recorded calls and their use to lure an endangered species can be illegal.

Making notes:
Try to use the correct terms to describe a bird in your notes. Some common ones to use in addition to "head," "eye," or "wing," are labeled on the European Starling (right) and Northern Goshawk (below).

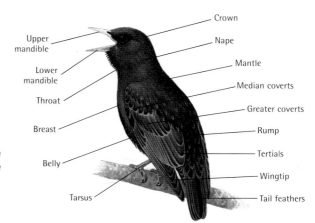

Upper mandible
Lower mandible
Throat
Breast
Belly
Tarsus

Crown
Nape
Mantle
Median coverts
Greater coverts
Rump
Tertials
Wingtip
Tail feathers

field, but do your best. Try to get an idea of the bird's basic shape and its bulk. Is it a slim, lightweight, elegant bird, or a big, heavy, lumbering bird? Also take note of the proportions of its body parts in relation to each other. Does it have a large head with a long neck, bill, and legs? Or is the bird round-bodied, short-tailed, and short-legged? Try to get as much of an overall impression as you can when you spot a

new or strange bird, including the way it moves and behaves. Is it walking quickly, hopping, or sitting still? Does it dash from bush to bush, or spend many minutes flying around over a field? If the bird is in a bush, does it sit quietly or is it constantly in motion, slipping through the foliage to hop from branch to branch? Does the bird sit and pick its food from the nearest twig or leaf, or does it hang upside down to reach

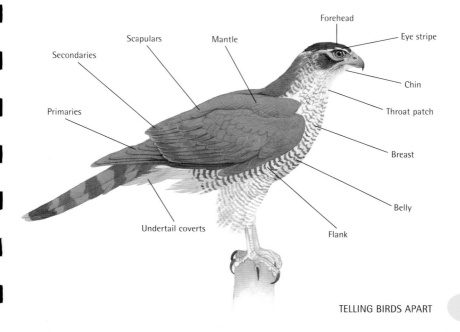

Secondaries
Primaries
Scapulars
Mantle
Forehead
Eye stripe
Chin
Throat patch
Breast
Belly
Undertail coverts
Flank

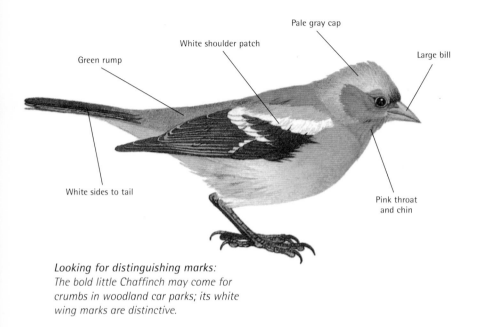

Green rump

White shoulder patch

Pale gray cap

Large bill

White sides to tail

Pink throat and chin

Looking for distinguishing marks:
The bold little Chaffinch may come for
crumbs in woodland car parks; its white
wing marks are distinctive.

around for its food? Is it alone or is it with other birds of the same or a different species?

Too often bird-watching beginners focus on just one or two points that are immediately obvious—such as a white patch on the body, or a yellow tinge to the wing—and ignore everything else, expecting that this will be enough to make an accurate identification. Usually, they will be disappointed. It is important to get as much information as you can. As you become more experienced, try to use the correct terms to describe the parts of a bird in your notes, including the tracts of feathers such as primaries and wing coverts. This will allow you to be more precise when describing what you have seen, and you will become fluent in the common language of bird-watchers.

RECOGNIZING OLD FRIENDS

Eventually, the wealth of information you gather will allow you to identify common birds with ease. For example, sparrows feed on the ground and fly away fast and straight to the nearest bush if they are disturbed, while swallows hunt insects in the air and fly in a relaxed, flowing manner, rarely stopping to perch. Thrushes feed on the ground, hopping and running, and stopping to look and listen, or probe the ground with their bill. Goldfinches feed in little groups in the tops of thistles, flitting from flower to flower. Pigeons seem to shuffle along and sit on rooftops for minutes at a time, while kestrels sit on open posts and treetops, coming to the ground only to capture their prey. All of these impressions will soon become familiar and gradually you will be able to recognize what "kind" of bird you are looking at. You can then start to pay closer attention to finer details: observing colors and patterns in plumage and listening to bird sounds. Experienced bird-watchers often do not need these finer details to identify a bird. They will see a bird fly across a field or perch in a bush and be able to name it simply because "that is what it looks like." With some practice, you will be able to do the same.

Identifying birds becomes easier as they become more familiar. It is like spotting a friend on a busy street: you do not have to check the color of the eyes or the shape of the nose, you simply know who it is. However, if you are trying to find someone you have never seen before, and have just a photograph as a reference point, smaller details become more important. Bird-watching works in a similar way. At first you will be looking for all the specific markings of a bird illustrated in a field guide, but eventually you will be able to see the same bird fly by and identify it on sight.

Using your eyes and ears: This adult male redpoll has a striking pink breast, but juveniles lack pink, and you need to look carefully for the black chin. Their calls can also help identify them.

Red cap

Tiny bill

Buff wingbar

Black chin

Plain brown tail

Streaked flank

TAKING NOTES AND MAKING SKETCHES

A notebook used to be part of every bird-watcher's outdoor kit. Now most bird-watchers use a digital camera fixed to a telescope to record what they see. Nevertheless, a notebook is exceptionally useful and is an ideal way to remember details about the birds you watch.

If you see something unusual when bird-watching, try to describe it in your notebook as thoroughly as possible. It is difficult to remember everything by memory alone, especially if you want to look up a bird in a book later to identify what you saw. Did the bird have pale brown legs and a buff band on the tail, or did you only read these things in the book? Were there four white spots on the wingtip or just three? It quickly becomes impossible to remember.

TAKE GOOD NOTES

If possible, write everything down while you are still watching the bird. You can scribble down your own shorthand and expand on it later. If you get details wrong you can change them as you watch the bird and get a better view. You might write down "black bill" and later change it to "dark brown bill with paler base," or "eyes looked dark" might become "brown

Mallard: Even on a common bird like this, the pattern is hard to describe without at least a few specialist terms to pinpoint colors, but they are easy to learn.

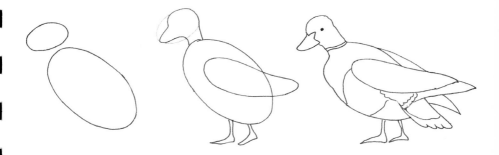

Sketching a duck: Start with a rough idea of shapes and proportions, then add shape, then colors and patterns.

eyes with paler ring" once you see the bird more closely. Do the best you can, but aim for as detailed an observation as possible.

You never know what crucial feature will help you identify a bird later, so make sure you write everything down. It can be helpful to make a sketch and label all the bird's features. This will make it clear what details are missing—perhaps you haven't labeled the legs, and this will prompt you to get a better look. Making a sketch forces you to look—closely, and properly. You can't draw the right pattern of streaks if you haven't seen them; you're not likely to get the head pattern right if you don't specifically choose to note head-pattern characteristics. Approach bird identification systematically, and know bird anatomy with an awareness of potential patterns of plumage and shapes of head, bill, wings, and tail.

If you are faced with a complicated bird, you can work at studying the details, noting them down, and putting them in a sketch, however crude it might be. Not only will you have to look at the bird carefully to get it right, but you will remember so much more about it, even months later.

Taking a bird's picture gives you a quick reference, but fixes little in your mind. A photograph is a record of a tiny moment: it may not be as "true" as you think. How often do you take a photograph of someone and find it doesn't really look right—perhaps they moved, or blinked, or turned away at the crucial moment. A photograph of a bird can be just as inaccurate. A drawing, or a written description, made as the bird moves and feeds, flies, and preens, will be a much more complete record than a moment caught by the camera. Of course, you may do both, but don't neglect the old-fashioned notebook and drawing.

HOW TO MAKE A SKETCH

Even if you are not a skilled artist, any drawing is better than none. Use rough egg shapes to get the basic idea of a head and body—as near as you can get to the right proportions. Is the body elongated horizontally, or vertically? Is it round or thin? Add wings, a tail, legs, and a bill as well as you can. Now put labels on all the features, making short notes with lines pointing to the position on the sketch. Make more sketches as you get a better view of the bird or see it from different angles.

SOUNDS

Bird calls and songs are crucial in helping you to identify a species. Bird-watchers also use them to locate birds, many finding more birds by using their ears than by using their eyes.

You can buy CDs containing recordings of bird sounds, but learning them directly from the bird that makes them is more effective, as it puts the sound into context and makes it more memorable. The best situation is to see the bird actually making the noise; then you know for certain what noise a species makes and are more likely to remember it later.

You may find it helpful to write down what a bird call sounds like. Use simple words or syllables to describe how the call sounds to you, such as tchew, twit, sweep, or chirrup. Add descriptions of the noise, such as liquid, metallic, sharp, hard, soft, silky, or abrupt. Many bird calls are difficult to describe because they consist of an extended vowel sound without a hard consonant—but do your best.

You can add a clue to the rise and fall and inflection of a call by drawing a line above it. For example, you can use a thick line that tapers out to indicate a call that fades away, or make the line bend up or down to show the rise and fall in pitch of the call. If you need to refer to a book or CD when you get home, these efforts can help you to remember what you heard.

TAKE NOTES RIGHT AWAY
Remember, once you have read a description of a bird, or looked at a photograph or a painting, or listened to a CD, it is more difficult to remember exactly what you originally saw or heard—details may become obscured. Once you have gone home, you cannot look at the live bird again to check something—so take notes and make sketches while you can. You will not regret it.

KEEPING A DIARY

Most bird-watchers like to keep some sort of log of the birds they have seen. Those who began bird-watching before personal computers were commonly used probably kept a simple written diary, a card index, or perhaps merely a life-list of birds they have seen. Many people who are starting out today will prefer to keep computerized records. However, there are pros and cons for every system and none, save perhaps for a sophisticated computer program, is perfect.

A daily bird-watching diary is useful. Important things to note include the date of the observations, the time, your location, perhaps the weather, and a list of birds you see. You can liven your diary up with the names of your companions, or note the day you first used your new binoculars. A good diary is far more than a basic list of birds—it is also a personal story that can include your thoughts, observations, and excitement at the best (or worst) of times.

In some special circumstances (if, for example, you are keeping detailed reports at a nature reserve), you might note everything you see. Usually, though, this becomes tedious and repetitive, and you will instead be more selective. By neglecting details, however, you risk losing good data on birds that are common now, but might not always be so. There has to be a compromise: keeping notes should add enjoyment to your hobby, not make it a chore, but it should also be useful.

The more you bird-watch, the more you will learn what is worth writing down and what is not. You will, after all, be keeping these notes for yourself, as a rule. They will be private rather than public records. You should send in all the significant and useful notes to a local or county bird recorder, to add to the official record. To do this easily, you may need a system that allows you to find all your notes from one location or all your notes on a particular species. This is where a card index works better than a daily diary. A computer log, on which you can search for specific words, is obviously the most efficient option. While a card index is helpful for finding all your sightings of any one species, it fails to tell you what you saw at a particular place or on a specific day, and it does not bring back memories, or record the atmosphere, in the way that a daily log does. And for many people, a computer diary isn't as "friendly" as a paper one.

THE PROS AND CONS

Do you want to keep the notebooks you take out bird-watching with you? Or do you prefer a more permanent record, written up in an exercise book, or typed onto a computer? You can, of course, keep both, but space becomes a problem over the years. In the end, you will find your own preferred method, but think about what you want from a notebook and try to make it practical—get it to work for you.

	PROS	CONS
Desktop computer	Quick, easy searches Compact Programs can sort information	Not portable Cannot use it in the field
Index cards	Easy reference Can categorize according to species, location, etc.	Impersonal and unevocative Takes up space
Notebook	Portable User-friendly Personal and evocative	Takes up space Can be difficult to find information

TAKING PHOTOGRAPHS

A camera is a great bird-watching tool, whether or not you use a notebook. It is difficult to take high-quality, close-up pictures of birds that are good enough to publish—that demands expensive gear and lots of time and effort. You can, however, take record shots easily. These can help you to identify birds later.

The best type of camera for bird photography is a single-lens reflex (SLR). These cameras let you see the same image through the viewfinder as will be recorded on the film or on your digital media card. The image you see is reflected into the viewfinder by a mirror, which flips out of the way when you push the shutter button, so that the image can be recorded. You can use different types of lenses on SLR cameras, including wide-angle, which have a very short focal length, and telephoto, which have a very long focal length. Telephoto lenses magnify, but generally do not give as good a close-up view as a telescope. To get the best bird pictures, you have to get close to the subject.

GETTING CLOSE
There are two ways to get close: either stalk the bird and get close to it by using good fieldcraft, or use a blind, so that the bird comes near to you without suspecting you are there. Many bird reserves have excellent blinds that let you get a close-up look at birds. You can also try building your own. You will need a lightweight but rigid framework covered in a camouflaged or possibly earth-tone fabric, tied so that it does not flap in the wind. For a more permanent structure, you might add camouflage materials, such as twigs, leaves, and turf. You need a way in—some sort of door—and a flap through which to extend your camera lens. The lens will often scare birds, so you may need to camouflage it somehow.

You can lure some birds—mainly common garden birds—closer by putting out food. Try to place food behind an object so that it will be hidden in the picture—you don't want all the birds in your photos to be eating peanuts or picking up mealworms or pieces of cake.

Stalking birds is also good fun and helps you learn more about birds. Garden birds can be surprisingly flighty and difficult to approach if they know you are watching them. Yet some really wild species, such as wading birds that have been reared in the Arctic, far from humans, might be remarkably naïve and almost ignore you, as long as you move

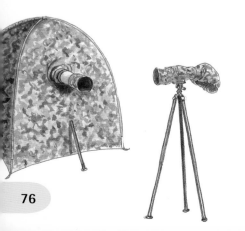

Hide: Even a simple blind, or hide, can keep you hidden, but you must stay quiet.

Digital camera

Tripod

Digital camera-telescope: Digital cameras are easily adapted for use on a telescope. For the best results, use a tripod.

slowly, smoothly, quietly, and not directly toward them. You may have difficulty getting close to an adult, but a juvenile—a young Ruff, say, or a Purple Sandpiper—might allow you almost within touching distance at times. You may be the first human they have seen.

GOOD PHOTOGRAPH STRATEGIES

Film and film processing are expensive and used less and less, but are still preferred over digital methods by some photographers. Digital cameras have become more common, and once you have the equipment, the pictures are practically free. You can shoot many, even hundreds, of pictures of the same bird, a practice that would be out of the question if using color film. You can also store digital pictures electronically, enhance them on a computer, and e-mail them to friends.

Digital cameras can be used to take shots through a telescope fitted with a small inexpensive adapter. The quality can be surprisingly good, giving you close-ups that you may have only dreamed of. Even if the pictures are not of professional standard, you can still impress your friends and document your feathered ones.

For the best results, a tripod is essential: nothing ruins photographs more than "handshake," or the jerk of the shutter, which blurs the image. A tripod helps keep the whole kit rigid and you can get a much sharper result. However, a tripod can be bulky and awkward, especially if you are stalking, so you might prefer to use the "wait and see" tactic. Sit by a pond or somewhere else that birds go to feed and simply see what turns up. This gives you a chance to get good pictures, and you will know in advance what you are going to see. If you have a specific target species, or want a picture of a particular bird, then stalking is often the best option.

PHOTOGRAPHY ETIQUETTE
When photographing birds, especially if you are trying to get a picture of a bird in the breeding season or you have a rare migrant or unidentified bird in sight, remember that the welfare of the bird is much more important than either your picture or your identification. Do not disturb birds, and do not chase them, and be aware of and courteous to other birders or photographers who may also be looking at the same bird.

CHOOSING AND USING BINOCULARS

Apart from a field guide illustrating the area's local birds, the only equipment a bird-watcher needs is a pair of binoculars. Despite all the codes and numbers used to describe them, binoculars are not difficult to use. Their shape, size, and weight are crucial if you use them a lot. A good pair will last a lifetime, so choose carefully and get the best you can afford.

Recommending a particular make and model of binoculars is not easy, because different shapes and sizes suit different people and manufacturers are constantly improving their products and coming out with new ones. Some people prefer to push the eyepieces tightly against their eyes, while others hold them farther away. Still others wear glasses and have different preferences. Some binoculars might bang against the bridge of your nose, or be too big and heavy, or too small and narrow. For bird-watching, a small, lightweight pair is ideal, but above all, it is important to make sure that binoculars are comfortable to use. They should "fit" your hands and the region around the eyes, so comfort largely depends on personal preference and the size and shape of your hands and face.

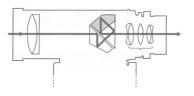

Roof prism: This design is the more modern and efficient type of binoculars.

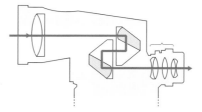

Porro prism: Light is reflected through a prism before reaching the eyepiece.

KEEP THEM CLEAN!
Eyepieces are often smeared with sunscreen, insect repellent, or make-up, and the larger lenses become dirty. Insect repellent can also damage the coating of lenses. When cleaning, avoid rubbing because it damages the lens coating and may grind in dirt, scratching the lens itself. Blow away dirt and dust, then gently brush the lens with a soft cloth designed for lens cleaning. Do not use a shirt or handkerchief, or any tissue paper other than specially made lens paper. It is always best to use a liquid lens cleaner with your lens cloth.

Roof prism binoculars

TYPES OF BINOCULARS

Binoculars come in two basic types: the roof prism, which looks straight-sided and slim, and the porro prism, which looks "step-sided" and has much wider front lenses (objective lenses) than eyepieces (ocular lenses). The roof prism is the more efficient system, but you may not notice a difference in the images it magnifies. They are also smaller and lighter in weight, and you can get compact or miniature models, but smaller binoculars let in less light and are less useful in low-light conditions. Try both types at a camera or optics store before making a decision.

One thing to keep in mind: porro prism binoculars have an external focusing mechanism—the front lenses move in and out on a greased rod when the viewer focuses on something. That grease is exposed to dust in the air. Over time, the grease becomes saturated with dust and dirt, making focusing more difficult or even impossible. Roof prism binoculars, on the other hand, have an internal focusing mechanism and therefore do not have any external moving parts that will become gummed up with grease.

Porro prism binoculars

POWER AND LENS SIZE

The magnification level (the number of times that an object will be enlarged) and the diameter of the larger lenses (in millimeters) of binoculars is always specified: 10x40 binoculars, for example, magnify the object by 10 times and have 40 mm lenses. For bird-watchers, a magnification, or "power," between 7 and 10 is generally suitable. However, the higher the power, the more difficult it will be to hold them steady—every movement of the hand is magnified as much as the image. You will need a bright image if you are to accurately identify birds. Larger front lenses allow more light in, and the higher the binoculars' power, the larger the lenses need to be to show the magnified picture brightly.

When choosing binoculars, divide the diameter of the front lenses (the second number) by the magnification (the first number) to get the diameter of the "exit pupil"—the bright beam of light that exits the eyepiece. There is no point to having an exit pupil that is larger than the pupil of your eye, as any

CLOSE FOCUS

Many binoculars do not allow you to focus on objects closer than about 15-20 feet (4.5-6 m). Binoculars that focus at closer distances allow you to scrutinize difficult-to-identify flowers across a ditch or butterflies across the garden pond. Test the binoculars for close focus before you buy.

extra light will be wasted. At its largest, your pupil will be about 7 mm, but in sunlight it is much smaller.

Binoculars with a 7x50 setting can be brighter still in shady conditions (the difference will not be noticeable on a sunny day). Roof prism binoculars, though, are so good, generally, that you can get away with 10x40 or 10x42 and still get a bright view. Compact types—8x25 or even 10x25—made by a good manufacturer can be very good, except in dull-light conditions, and are remarkably light and pocket-size.

FOCUSING BINOCULARS

Once you have selected your binoculars, you must first learn how to focus and adjust them to fit the distance between your eyes and to accommodate the differences in the performance of your right and left eyes.

The first adjustment to make takes account of the distance between your eyes, which varies greatly in different people. Modern binoculars are constructed so that the two optical barrels pivot around a central axis, allowing the distance between the eyepieces to be adjusted. First, push the barrels closely together. Then point them toward a distant object, raise them to your eyes, and slowly increase the space between the barrels until you see a maximum field of view. This happens when the individual fields of view of the two barrels (the separate images seen by your two eyes) appear to merge and form an oval or circle. The binoculars are now adjusted to fit the distance between your eyes.

Next you must focus the two barrels separately, to take account of the variations in sight between your eyes—even people with good vision usually do not have equally matched sight in both eyes. Once you have made these adjustments (see Adjusting for Visual Acuity, facing page), your binoculars are ready to use for observation.

Practice using your binoculars until you can raise them to your eyes

EYEPIECES

Some brands of binoculars have eyepieces that click into two or three positions or that have extendable or foldable rubber eye cups, and you may find that one suits you more than another. If you wear glasses, having a rubber eye cup protects your eyeglasses, and being able to fold it back on itself allows you to increase the size of the exit pupil, thus enhancing your field of view.

Central focusing wheel

Step 1: Adjust the central focusing wheel until an image appears—it does not need to be sharply focused.

Left, non-adjustable eyepiece   Right, adjustable eyepiece

Adjustment ring

Step 2: Cover the adjustable (in this case, the right) lens, and use the central wheel to focus the left eyepiece on a sharp-edged object. Then cover the left lens and use the individual eyepiece control to focus the right eyepiece on the same object—do not touch the central wheel.

ADJUSTING FOR VISUAL ACUITY

Binoculars can be adjusted to accommodate the differences in your eyes' performance. You have to adjust this setting before you use the binoculars and then keep it in place in order to continue achieving the sharpest focus. On most models the adjustment is made by moving one eyepiece independently of the other using an adjustment ring, which may be mounted around the eyepiece or in front of the central focusing ring. On some models it is the right eyepiece that is adjustable, on others the left. In a few models, the adjustment is made to one of the front lenses.

Step 3: Now use the central wheel only to focus on different objects. Check the right eyepiece occasionally to maintain the correct balance between eyes.

without moving your head—this will enable you to keep the bird in sight and avoid disturbing it. Looking directly at the bird (not at the binoculars), raise the binoculars smoothly to your eyes. Swinging your head from side to side with your binoculars in place to get the bird in view is not the way to do it. You can practice this exercise using any object. There are binoculars on the market with image-stabilization technology, but, besides being heavier and more expensive, these are not really suitable when tracking moving objects.

SPOTTING SCOPES AND TRIPODS

Spotting scopes are handy if you need a magnification of 15–20x or higher. A large lens (which gives a brighter image) increases the size and weight of a spotting scope, so make sure it is practical to use. If you want a large lens, go for a 20x60 lens (the first number indicates the magnification of the lens, the second its diameter in mm) or 30x70.

Powerful scopes will be heavy and cumbersome, rendering them impractical in areas such as woods, where birds are too close or move too quickly to observe with a large lens. But a spotting scope can be invaluable at a reservoir or estuary, and may be good fun even in the garden.

TRIPODS AND ACCESSORIES

To hold a scope steady, you will need a tripod for outdoors or a mounting bracket that fits on the window of an automobile. The window bracket can also be used, with some modification, in a blind. In general, however, you will need a full-size tripod with extendable legs. You can often use a tripod without the legs extended, when sitting on a bank, for example, which is usually more comfortable and more stable.

A comfortable shoulder strap is a great accessory for carrying the spotting scope and tripod around. You can also buy a fabric case that protects the scope from the elements and helps camouflage it, but the case is not essential—a little rain will not hurt a good scope and the scope would be of no use in a heavy rain.

A spotting scope is ideal for watching birds at 20 yards or more; even a sparrow 20 yards away looks fantastic through one. But consider

Straight telescope: It is easier to pick up birds through a direct-line from the eyepiece, but it may be awkward to use if the bird is high up.

carefully whether you want one or not. If your budget does not stretch to a pair of binoculars and a spotting scope, just get the binoculars. They are more practical and versatile.

Angled telescope: The angled eyepiece makes it harder at first to locate a bird, but is more comfortable to use.

Spotting scopes are either "straight" or "angled." A straight eyepiece makes it easier to pick up the bird, but you might have to position yourself awkwardly to look through it. Angled eyepieces can be used more easily, on a lower tripod, and are much better for looking at objects against the sky. Eyepieces are a matter of personal preference, so try one out before you buy.

Resist buying inexpensive spotting scopes with tiny lenses that give a dim image and a tiny field of view. However, some small "travel scopes" are now extremely good. In general, you pay for what you get.

CHOOSING A LENS

Field of view is a fundamental quality of a lens—it is the width of the area visible, measured in meters, at 1,000 meters range. The larger the figure, the wider the field, and the more useful the lens for bird-watching and general use. A wide-angle lens is indicated by the letters W, WA, or WW.

Fluorite lenses reduce the blue and red "color fringes" seen around objects of strong contrast, such as twigs against a light sky. In other words, they give the viewer a cleaner, crisper, more correctly colored view. Many spotting scopes and binoculars now use these lenses.

Several more acronyms are used to describe certain lens qualities that are less easy to measure or define: ED refers to "extra low dispersion." HG usually means "high grade," but is a vague term applied by the maker to better-quality ranges. HD can mean "high definition" or "highly durable." The best thing you can do is ignore these acronyms and simply try out some scopes and read some reviews before buying.

CLOTHING AND OTHER EQUIPMENT

A bird-watcher needs very little equipment, but there will inevitably be some extra gear that appeals to certain people. Bird-watching is a hobby that has no rules. The gear you decide to use is a matter of personal choice.

It is best to use a notebook that fits in a pocket and is securely bound or spiral-bound. Although most people use a ballpoint pen, a pencil is better in case it rains. Felt-tip pens are not the best choice as they smudge in wet weather and soak through the paper.

ELECTRONIC AIDS

It is possible to view a field guide electronically on a tiny hand-held computer. These are particularly helpful if they play bird calls and songs well enough to be recognizable—not all do. More often than not, computers are frustrating to use in the field—they are more for show than for practical use. You can see only one bird at a time on a hand-held screen, and perhaps only one age or sex. It is much easier to flick through the pages of a book until you find what you want. When trying to identify species, a book can help you to make comparisons and rule out certain birds much more easily. Although you can key in notes and even make sketches on a computer, a notebook gives you much greater freedom and speed, old-fashioned though it may be.

There are innumerable DVD and video guides that you can use at home, and these make marvelous additions to a field guide. You can also purchase massive handbooks on CD or DVD and bring up the contents of a dozen giant volumes on screen in a few moments. Modern bird-watchers have everything they need at their fingertips.

If you see a large number of birds—such as a flock of gulls or wading birds on an estuary—and wish to count them, or to record the proportion of males and females or adults and young, a tally counter is invaluable. By clicking it with a finger you can keep track of how many birds you see without having to remember numbers. For big flocks, just click every tenth bird and add a zero at the end. Or you can count males in your head, and females on the counter, without having to do it twice over.

A tape or CD player can be handy to listen to recordings outside, or to play bird calls to lure skulking birds from cover: but use this with great care and restraint, as it does disturb the birds.

You might like to make recordings yourself: you need a good recording machine and microphone, as well as either a parabolic reflector to focus sound onto the microphone or a good directional microphone (known as a "shotgun mike"). Seek specialist advice regarding a reliable product.

CLOTHING

Clothing is entirely a personal thing, but there are a few basic principles. You need to be comfortable: cool, or warm, or dry, depending on the conditions. It is important to keep your feet dry and your head warm. You lose a great deal of heat through your scalp, so a hat is a must in severe weather.

Modern clothing can be waterproof while still being lightweight and soft.

CHECKLIST WHEN YOU GO OUT

Priorities
- Binoculars
- Identification pocket guide
- Notebook and pencil
  (better than a pen if it rains)

Options
- Telescope
- Tripod with advanced movable/
  lockable head
- Mini travel scope for overseas trips
- PDA (personal digital assistant)
  hand-held computer, electronic
  field guide, and notebook
- Large-scale map
- Breathable waterproof clothing
- Umbrella and warm hat
- Hand warming gel packs
- A simple digital tally counter

Advanced options
- Camera—preferably SLR,
  preferably digital
- Camera adaptor for telescope
  to go "digiscoping"
- Computer-based photo storage,
  editing, and management system
- Laptop for downloading pictures
  on trips away from home

- Portable photographer's blind (hide)
- Sound enhancement/amplifying
  system to ease high-frequency
  hearing impairment
- Sound recording system,
  with parabolic reflector
  (for serious bird-watchers)
- Expanded library of books
- Set of bird Web sites added
  to your Internet favorites
- A place on a bird ringing
  (banding) training course
- Subscriptions to scientific
  and specialist journals

Back home
- "Master" logbook for recording
  your notes—paper or computer
- Handbook of birds
- Interactive CD-ROM version
- DVD/video bird guides
- Sound guide CD
- Local, national, and world checklists
- Set of local bird reports
- Set of national bird journals
- Subscription to local bird club
- Subscription to national
  conservation body
- "Where to watch birds" guides

Try to get something that doesn't rustle: a soft, breathable fabric is best. If you are going to spend a lot of time in the sun, modern fabrics that incorporate protection against ultraviolet light, combined with sunscreens, offer the most effective protection. Large pockets for guides and notebooks are useful, as are gloves with open fingers that allow you to sketch, take notes, and focus your binoculars during cold weather.

Some bird-watchers wear what looks like army gear, even on a hot sunny day out in the open. It isn't necessary: birds will see you long before you see them. However, it is best to avoid whites, bright pinks, and similar striking colors in favor of pale buff, brown, green, and blue. Only if you are in a blind or stalking a bird really close, for photography perhaps, do you really need to try to look invisible.

FARTHER AFIELD

Bird-watching from your window, looking at garden birds, is a good way to start, and garden birds will keep you amused and fascinated for a lifetime. But no doubt you will soon want to explore farther and see different kinds of birds. Your daily routine will reveal only a tiny fraction of the birds out there. Birds are everywhere and you will want to know what species you are looking at.

Look through a field guide and you will see birds you have hardly dreamed of, and they may be close by. If you want to see new birds, the first thing to do is to head for water. Try the beach, a flooded gravel pit, or a reservoir. Water and the water's edge provide habitats for a huge number and variety of birds.

WATCHING AROUND WATER

Gravel pits tend to be quite deep and steep-sided, so they are ideal for several kinds of ducks, especially diving ducks such as Ring-necked Ducks, Redheads, and Buffleheads, but not necessarily for those that potter about in the shallows such as Green-winged Teal,

and shovelers. Gravel pits often contain grebes and perhaps geese or swans. Reservoirs in steep-sided valleys between high hills tend to be cold, deep, and acidic, and have few birds on the whole. But those created on lowland farmland in wide, shallow valleys can be exceptional. The shores become muddy, and any small drop in water level is likely to reveal vast areas of mud, which becomes overgrown in the summer but flooded again in autumn, releasing a superabundance of seeds for winter wildfowl to eat.

The shallow sides attract wading birds on their spring and autumn migrations, too. These can be some of the most exciting birds you can find—not only are the common ones beautiful species that may be on their way to the Southern Hemisphere from the Arctic, but the chances of finding something quite rare are fairly good. The water's edge is excellent, too, for birds such as meadowlarks, pipits, finches, and various sparrows. Insects over the water attract early migrants, and flocks of

Canada Goose: Even common birds such as the Canada Goose have particular needs and take you away from your backyard—head for water to see this one.

swallows and swifts often gather there in bad weather, when food is hard to find elsewhere. Over the water, too, may be migrant terns, and from late summer to spring, there may well be a big nighttime roost of gulls flying in to find a safe place to sleep after feeding on local farmland or refuse tips.

Any area around these watery places is worth exploring. Willow thickets, bramble and scrub patches, reeds, and rushes are all likely to have interesting breeding birds and migrants that rely on the proximity to water to provide a reliable supply of insects.

On the coast the possibilities are endless. A rocky shore appeals to certain species, while a sandy one may be less rich in birds. But mud, especially in a big estuary, is a super-rich habitat with a fantastic supply of food, which is refreshed twice a day by the tide. As the tide falls, huge numbers of shorebirds of many kinds spread out over the flats. This can be challenging bird-watching, as birds are at long range and conditions are often difficult, but it can be remarkably rewarding. Often, too, there are roads—even urban promenades—that overlook wonderful places for birds in estuarine locations. A trip to the seashore to look for birds should be timed to arrive at low tide.

OTHER HABITATS

Woodlands are full of birds, but are often tricky places in which to bird-watch. Dense summer foliage makes things difficult and, in winter, birds are fewer and more concentrated in wandering flocks. It is best to go early in the day in spring, when everything is singing and the leaves are still sparse, or to wander patiently in winter until you come across a mixed flock, when things

Eastern Meadowlark: Some birds are widespread on farmland, others need old pastures or natural grasslands.

will suddenly be hectic for a minute or two before they pass by. For birds of prey, it is often best to stay outside the wood, preferably on a hill from which you can look out across the forest and watch for birds displaying over the forest in spring. Woodpeckers, warblers, thrushes, nuthatches, and creepers are typical woodland birds.

Scrublands are wide-open, sometimes bleak places, and birds can be few and far between except in spring and summer. You need to be patient. Walk slowly and carefully, checking bushes and thickets and looking overhead for passing birds of prey. Their special species make these habitats well worth the visit, but finding all their secrets may take time.

Mountains and hillsides have some special birds, but these are expansive habitats, and you must be sure you are safe—the weather can change dramatically. Take care, wear the right footwear, take food and drink, a map, and warm clothing. But do try to see some mountain birds if you can. It is often possible to do so from a roadside, but you might need to climb a hilltop or explore a valley: keep high and look over the lower areas. The Golden Eagle, Peregrine Falcon, and ptarmigans are highlights to seek out in the mountains.

MAKE YOUR BACKYARD A BIRD RESERVE

Transforming your yard into a refuge for wildlife is easy to do, is good fun, and brings great rewards. With a little effort, you can attract beautiful songbirds and other interesting wildlife to your yard, which the whole family can enjoy watching. Creating a bird sanctuary can help you unwind and relieve the stress of the working week.

Gardening practices that help wildlife, reduce chemicals in your yard, and conserve water also help to improve the quality of air, water, and soil throughout your neighborhood. Backyards can support wildlife all year round, but birds need your help most during the colder months and in the early spring when wild food is still scarce and winter supplies are already exhausted. Feeding wild birds is a popular hobby, second only to gardening in North America.

A SAFE ENVIRONMENT
Keeping your bird feeders clean is vitally important—unhygienic practices are more likely to lead to disease in the birds that feed in your garden. Placing them in the right place is also necessary if you want to keep birds safe from predators and other dangers (see How to Feed Birds in the Garden, pp. 48–49). Predation by household cats is a major cause of backyard bird deaths, and a study by the American Birding Association found cats to be significant killers of birds that come to feeders. A single domestic household cat can kill more than 100 birds and small mammals each year: even if one bird a month is killed in this way, it still translates to millions of birds being killed by pet cats throughout the U.S. Make sure you place feeders away from anywhere a cat can lie in ambush.

Window strikes are a frequent cause of injury or death to birds—reflections on a big window on a sunny day may create the illusion of an open space that birds may try to fly through. You should take measures to reduce the risk of window strikes. Simply relocating a feeder may help the problem. There are also many ways to disrupt reflections in windows, such as putting stickers on the windows or hanging netting or objects outside them. Shiny objects in particular are more likely to deter birds from approaching.

MAKING YOUR GARDEN HOSPITABLE
What kind of habitat do you have in your own backyard? A pile of brush may be unsightly, but it can help birds escape predators such as cats and Sharp-shinned Hawks. A good thick shrub or hedge can do the same. It should be within easy reach of the feeder, but not so close that a cat can leap out to pounce on a bird.

You should provide birds with water for drinking and bathing. If you do not have room for a pond, a birdbath will suffice, but make sure you keep it topped up with clean, fresh water. A small pond is by far a better option, though, if you are able to create one. It should be quite deep, and lined with old carpet beneath a layer of plastic or rubber pond liner. Also add a layer of earth. Or else you can simply buy an artificial pond. Make sure some of the pond's edges are shallow and slope gradually so that birds can walk in gently: they don't like having to plunge straight in out of their depth. Add a selection of native waterside plants, but leave some open space, too, around the pond edge. It is best not to have fish in a garden pond, as they eat insects and tadpoles. This set-up is better suited for a wildlife garden.

As well as setting up a selection of feeders, you should provide other food sources for birds: plants and trees with fruits and berries, or flowers that attract plenty of insects. If you have the space, dead trees or branches help birds such as woodpeckers to find food and nest sites.

If you want to get serious about backyard wildlife, you can register with the Backyard Wildlife Habitat Program with the National Wildlife Federation, which acknowledges the efforts of people who garden for wildlife, gives personal registration certificates, and adds wildlife gardens to the national register of backyard wildlife habitats.

Birdbath: Birds need to bathe regularly to keep in good shape, even in cold weather.

Bird populations are not only the measure of the changing fortunes of wild birds worldwide, they are also seen as an indication of the health of the environment as a whole. In the U.K., for example, the overall trend for countryside bird numbers is one of the official government indicators of the sustainability and quality of life.

In the U.K., there is a long history of bird-watching as a hobby and large numbers of volunteer bird-watchers who take part in census and monitoring activities. For more than a century, the Christmas Bird Count across North America has helped to define trends in winter bird populations. The North American Breeding Bird Survey helps to chart changes in numbers of summer birds.

MAKING UP THE NUMBERS

Population trends of birds in these countries are monitored annually, using both professional staff and hundreds, or thousands, of volunteer bird-watchers who undertake regular counts and census work. In some European countries with a large and well-organized bird-watching population, such as the Netherlands, such census work is now possible, but in most

Madagascar Fish-eagle:
This species is now
critically endangered due
to a variety of threats.

countries, even within Europe, census work is far less complete and has a much shorter history, making the assessment of long-term trends much more difficult. In conservation—and especially in influencing governments and decision makers to take practical action—the hard facts produced by the national counts are priceless.

In Asia, monitoring of breeding and wintering species is still minimal, with so few bird-watchers spread over vast areas of the continent. Nevertheless, the gigantic losses of rainforest in Southeast Asia and Indonesia must have immense implications for numbers of breeding birds to the north. There are, however, detailed surveys of breeding birds in particular Southeast Asian forests. These show a great reduction in both numbers and variety of bird species when rainforest is changed to a monoculture of oil palm or rubber trees.

In Australia, there are detailed atlases of breeding birds and long-established counts of wintering birds, but coverage is perhaps

POOR SEED CROPS IN BRITISH COLUMBIA

Birds such as Common Redpolls vary from year to year as food supply alters. In 2006, a massive spruce crop in northern British Columbia attracted huge numbers of redpolls, White-Winged Crossbills, and Pine Grosbeaks. In southern British Columbia, though, the seed crop was poor, and birders reported the worst year in memory for these and other winter forest finches.

The highly social Pine Siskin moves around North America during winter, simply heading for wherever the most food is located. The British Columbia coast usually has the highest concentration of wintering Pine Siskins on the continent, but with poor seed crops in 2006 there were almost none. A Christmas Bird Count in Victoria, Canada, reported 68: in a good year they have 10,000.

predictably patchy in a country with such a sparse and scattered human population. Africa has even greater problems in monitoring its birds. Some countries, such as Kenya, Zimbabwe, and South Africa, have a fairly long and solid history of bird population monitoring and atlas work, but there are vast areas whose birds are still all but unknown.

GLOBAL TRENDS

Overall declines in bird populations are due mainly to two factors: habitat loss or degradation and, more recently, climate change (see Conservation, pp. 94–96). Flood prevention and drainage have caused declines in wetland birds for centuries—where lakes and reservoirs have been protected and floods allowed, some wintering geese and ducks have thrived. The outlook for these northern-breeding birds is bleak in the long term, as global climate change threatens to reduce the area of suitable breeding habitat of most. Many birds of the far north, or high altitudes, simply have nowhere left to go once

rising temperatures push them farther "uphill" or toward the Arctic.

In most developed countries, the intensification of agriculture has caused a downward turn in farmland bird numbers, as vast areas of bird- and flower-rich countryside are reduced to monotonous monocultures with little wildlife. Deforestation in the tropics, for example, and the change from native forest to plantations of exotic species, or monocultures of such plants as coffee, have put great stress on the North American woodland birds that migrate to Central and South America each winter.

The use of much more effective pesticides—including both insecticides, which directly affect the food supply of most birds in summer, and herbicides, which reduce the food of seed-eating birds, as well as the plants that create habitats for nesting and support insects and other invertebrates—has seen a widespread and often huge reduction in the amount of food available for birds in the countryside, and their numbers have plummeted as a result.

ENDANGERED BIRDS

Threats to birds are not new: they began in earnest in the age of mass migration and industrialization in the 19th century. As our world becomes even more urbanized and industrialized, and our land is intensively farmed, many birds will simply have nowhere to go. Habitats are steadily being converted to farmland, paved over for highways, or used to build factories, housing, retail, and tourism developments. Their related pollution and chemical toxins contaminate the land, water, and air. Below is a small selection of birds under threat. According to the 2006 IUCN Red List, there are currently 674 species that are classified as vulnerable, 351 as endangered, and 181 as critically endangered.

SOUTH & CENTRAL AMERICA

HYACINTH MACAW
Brazil, Bolivia, Paraguay
Endangered

YELLOW-HEADED
AMAZON PARROT
Mexico, Belize, Honduras, Guatemala
Endangered

ANDEAN FLAMINGO
Peru, Bolivia, Chile, Argentina.
Vulnerable

NORTH AMERICA

SALTMARSH
SHARP-TAILED SPARROW
Canada and USA
Vulnerable

BLACK-CAPPED VIREO
USA and Mexico
Vulnerable

CERULEAN WARBLER
Canada and USA
Vulnerable

CALIFORNIA CONDOR
USA and Mexico
Critically endangered

MOUNTAIN PLOVER
Canada, USA, and Mexico
Vulnerable

MARBLED MURRELET
Canada and USA
Endangered

AFRICA

MADAGASCAR
FISH-EAGLE
Madagascar
Critically endangered

AFRICAN PENGUIN
Namibia and South Africa
Vulnerable

SPOTTED GROUND-THRUSH
Kenya, Tanzania, South Africa, Malawi, Sudan, Democratic Republic of Congo
Endangered

Crested Ibis

Fi Fisheries-related injury   **🐾** Predators   **≈** Climate change   **P** Persecution

EUROPE

AQUATIC WARBLER
Central and eastern Europe
Vulnerable

SPANISH IMPERIAL EAGLE
Spain and Portugal
Vulnerable

GREAT BUSTARD
Western, central, and eastern Europe
Vulnerable

GREATER SPOTTED EAGLE
Central and eastern Europe
Vulnerable

BALEARIC SHEARWATER
Spain
Critically endangered

DALMATIAN PELICAN
Central and eastern Europe
Vulnerable

ASIA

INDIAN VULTURE
India and Pakistan
Critically endangered

CRESTED IBIS
China
Vulnerable

ORIENTAL STORK
Northern and southeastern Asia
Critically endangered

JAPANESE NIGHT-HERON
Northern and southeastern Asia
Critically endangered

*California
Condor*

SOUTHERN OCEANS

WANDERING ALBATROSS
Southern Oceans
Vulnerable

SPECTACLED PETREL
Southern Atlantic, Tristan da Cunha
Critically endangered

ROCKHOPPER PENGUIN
South Atlantic, Antarctica
Vulnerable

AUSTRALASIA

AUSTRALASIAN BITTERN
Australia and New Zealand
Endangered

GREAT SPOTTED KIWI
New Zealand
Vulnerable

KAKAPO
New Zealand
Critically endangered

CONSERVATION

Two major threats to birds loom large: habitat loss or degradation and climate change. Human-induced climate change threatens to put thousands of species closer to the edge of extinction in the next few decades. As conditions naturally change, birds will often adapt, but climate change may be at a much faster rate than would naturally be the case. For birds and other wild creatures, adapting is a race between life and death.

This can be seen in Europe and North America even at quite local levels. For example, some species rely on the scrubby vegetation and sandy soil of open heath or scrubland. As the climate warms, conditions for scrubland development begin to shift north: but, the species associated with such a specialized habitat cannot simply "move north" as the climate warms up. The same holds true when North American prairie land is lost to agriculture. The greatest threat to the Prairie Chicken is the conversion of its habitat to cropland.

DOING THE RIGHT THING?

It is essential to foresee the changes and attempt to create "stepping stones" and corridors of suitable scrub or grassland habitat, so that the wildlife can move gradually to new areas. But creating new habitats, or restoring areas previously lost to neglect or different land uses, is hugely expensive and demanding. It must be remembered, too, that birds are merely part of the ecosystem: all the essential plants, insects, soil invertebrates, reptiles, and other life must move, too.

Some small birds rely on a "flush" of green, energy-rich caterpillars in spring, to feed to their chicks. Climate change has in some cases encouraged such caterpillars to appear earlier in spring, or thrown local situations into such turmoil that they no longer appear in such numbers. Birds, adapting less rapidly and still nesting at their usual times, now find too few caterpillars at the crucial time and many pairs have chicks dying of starvation in the nest.

Another worrying sign of the effects of climate change is seen in seabirds in the North Atlantic and associated seas. Many species, including kittiwakes, guillemots, and Arctic Terns, rely on sand eels as food. Sand eels in turn feed on plankton, which thrives in

Osprey: In the U.K., the Osprey's story is a conservation classic and its population is recovering. In other parts of the world the bird is more common.

NEW PREDATORS

A simplistic view of the relationship between predators and prey is that it exists in a neat balance: after all, if predators greatly reduced the numbers of their prey, they would no longer have any food. This idea is sound when it is applied to a predator that preys on only one species or a limited range of prey. But many predators are opportunistic and can survive by eating many kinds of prey. If one kind is reduced, they can switch to something else. So, in certain circumstances and in localized areas, predators can reduce numbers of at least some of their prey and the interrelationships are complex.

But what happens when a new species, a potential new predator, is introduced? Any inherent balance is upset. Humans have been responsible for the direct and indirect introduction of invasive species of animals and plants as they have traveled the world, and if the new species becomes established, the results can be catastrophic. Not only will the introduced species bring new diseases and parasites, it will kill indigenous species or compete for land and food. Alien species have been responsible for the extinction of at least 65 species in the last five centuries, and are particularly destructive to island species.

This is the most dangerous threat to birds after habitat destruction and over-exploitation. Invasive species find it easier to adapt to habitats that have been fragmented or degraded. Globalization and climate change is making the situation worse: as we travel more, we increase the risk of further contamination, and warmer temperatures allow some parasites to increase their range.

Peregrine Falcon

clean, cold water. As sea temperatures have risen, especially in the North Sea, the plankton seems to have been forced to shift north: so, in parts of the seabirds' range, there are now too few sand eels to feed to their young.

A CHANGING LANDSCAPE

Habitat loss has marched side by side with human development and population increase for many centuries, and continues unabated. The loss of rainforests, for example, remains a critical and hugely damaging threat

to birds worldwide, not just those that breed in the forests but also those that breed in Europe and North America, but migrate to such forests in winter. Changes in forests can be dramatic, even without total destruction: for example, the development of coffee plantations has affected numbers of northern migrants, which are no longer able to survive in such numbers during winter months. Oil palm, rubber, and other plants that have replaced vast areas of natural forest have, in all detailed studies, proved to be less rich

Rough-Legged Hawk: Birds of prey are at the top of a food chain and are usful indicators of environmental health.

in birds than the original habitat that they have replaced.

The loss of farmlands, woodlands, scrublands, and wetlands continues as industrial and residential developments eat up vast areas of countryside in every developed country. Habitat fragmentation—in which woodland, for example, is sliced in two by a road or urban development—is continuing to cause severe damage.

THREAT FROM INDUSTRY

In Europe, there are fears, too, that countries entering the European Union will soon change to a more intensive, and more damaging farming regime, following the disastrous path that has already seen farmland birds decline dramatically in those countries with industrial-style farming. Furthermore,

Golden Eagle: Many eagles are killed by wind-powered turbine generators, an unexpected hazard of recent years.

the universal use of chemical toxins or pesticides in agriculture has had a catastrophic affect on wildlife.

The threat at sea is no less great than on land. Fisheries-related industry degrades and destroys the environment and habitat—oil spills, infrastructure development, disturbance—and seabirds suffer from death from entanglement in fishing nets and by fish hooks. In a few countries, birds are used as bait.

A SILVER LINING?

Such problems are but a few of the threats facing wildlife now: solutions are available, but need greater commitment, both from the public and from governments. A combination of public pressure, active lobbying of international authorities, detailed ecological research, and political action can help turn the situation around.

However, we are in a greater position now to learn from our mistakes: the Snowy Egret flourished as soon as plume hunting was banned, and the Peregrine Falcon is making a comeback after the pesticides that pushed it to the brink of extinction were prohibited. Nature reserves and ecotourism can help to protect habitats and their specialized species, as well as serve as an educational tool.

BIRD CATALOG

The pages that follow feature over 50 common birds
that can be found in the eastern United States. Those
that can be seen in and around gardens and towns
are examined, along with some that are easy to see up
close in locations such as a town park (especially if it
has a lake) or in nearby farmland. This catalog includes
illustrations and details that will help you to identify
these species: size, habitat, distribution during the
breeding season and during winter, and preferred foods.
Three of the species here—the Eurasian Starling, House
Sparrow, and Rock Pigeon—are non-native species
that were introduced to North America. Once you go
beyond the habitats described here, you will begin to
see many more species, and a more comprehensive
identification guide will be needed.

DOUBLE-CRESTED CORMORANT
Size 27 inches (69 cm)
Habitat Rivers, lakes, park lakes, coasts
Breeds Most of North America
Winters Pacific coast, Atlantic and Gulf coasts,
   North Carolina to Belize
Food Fish

A*s*

A*w* ♂

MALLARD
Size 16 inches (41 cm)
Habitat Water, especially freshwater,
   waterside areas
Breeds Almost all of North America
Winters Northern birds move south
Food Seeds, shoots, aquatic vegetation,
   invertebrates

AMERICAN COOT
Size 12 inches (30 cm)
Habitat Lakes, reservoirs, rivers,
   parks, ponds
Breeds Canada to Ecuador
Winters Resident in
   breeding areas
Food Aquatic plants and
   invertebrates

A*w*
A*s*

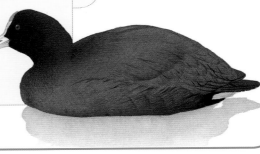

SHARP-SHINNED HAWK
Size 10–14 inches (25–36 cm); female larger
Habitat Woods, parks, gardens, farmland with trees
Breeds Canada south to northern Gulf states
Winters Northern U.S. southward
Food Small birds

AMERICAN KESTREL
Size 8 ½ inches (22 cm)
Habitat Parks, gardens, open fields, bushy
  areas, woodland edge
Breeds Most of North and South America
Winters Resident in breeding areas
Food Small rodents, insects, small birds

Aw
As
♂

RING-BILLED GULL
Size 16 inches (41 cm)
Habitat Lakes, quays and beaches, farmland
Breeds Canada, northern U.S.
Winters Coasts, southern U.S. to Gulf,
  Mexico, Cuba
Food Fish, scraps, worms

As

ROCK PIGEON
Size 11 inches (28 cm)
Habitat Towns, cities, quarries, cliffs,
  farmland, parks
Breeds Almost throughout North and
  South America
Winters Resident in breeding areas
Food Seeds and scraps

Aw
As

 J Juvenile   Feeds at birdtables   Feeds at hanging feeders   Uses nest boxes

Aw As

MOURNING DOVE
Size 10 ½ inches (27 cm)
Habitat Suburbia, woodland edge, farmland with trees
Breeds Southeastern Alaska and southern Canada south to Panama
Winters Resident in breeding range
Food Seeds and shoots

As

YELLOW-BILLED CUCKOO
Size 11 inches (28 cm)
Habitat Open woods, orchards, streamside trees
Breeds Almost throughout U.S.; rare in northwestern quarter
Winters South America
Food Insects, especially caterpillars

Aw As

EASTERN SCREECH-OWL 🏠
Size 8 inches (20 cm)
Habitat Woodlands, farmland with shelter belts
Breeds Southeastern Alaska southward to Mexico
Winters Resident in breeding areas
Food Rodents, small birds

Great Horned Owl

Aw
As

Size 20 inches (51 cm)
Habitat Forests, woodlands, thickets, open country with scattered trees
Breeds Alaska south throughout Americas
Winters Resident in breeding range
Food Rodents and larger mammals, birds

As

Chimney Swift

Size 5 inches (13 cm)
Habitat Open air throughout, nesting in hollow trees and chimneys
Breeds Eastern North America from southern Canada to Mexico
Winters South America
Food Flying insects

Ruby-throated Hummingbird

As
♂

Size 3 inches (7 ½ cm)
Habitat Gardens, woodland edges with flowers
Breeds Eastern North America from southern Canada to Gulf states
Winters Mexico and Central America
Food Nectar, tiny insects, spiders

Red-bellied Woodpecker

Aw
As
♂

Size 8 ½ inches (22 cm)
Habitat Woodlands, orchards, gardens, parks
Breeds Great Lakes; New England to Gulf States
Winters Resident in breeding areas
Food Insects, seeds, berries

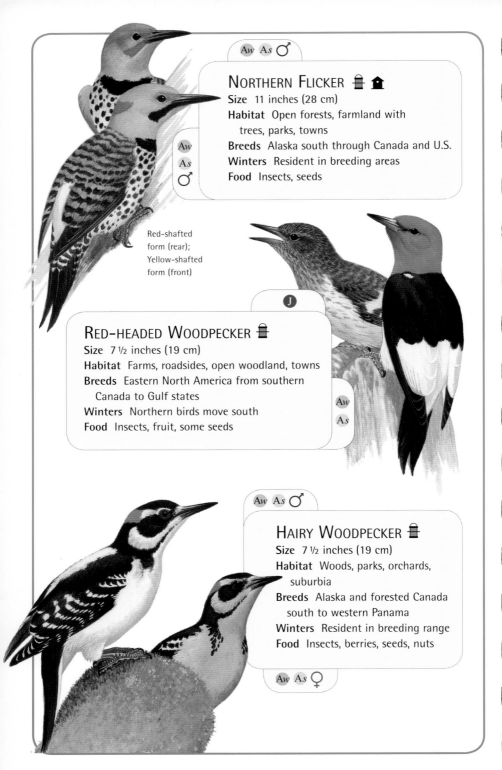

Northern Flicker

Size 11 inches (28 cm)
Habitat Open forests, farmland with trees, parks, towns
Breeds Alaska south through Canada and U.S.
Winters Resident in breeding areas
Food Insects, seeds

Red-shafted form (rear); Yellow-shafted form (front)

Red-headed Woodpecker

Size 7 ½ inches (19 cm)
Habitat Farms, roadsides, open woodland, towns
Breeds Eastern North America from southern Canada to Gulf states
Winters Northern birds move south
Food Insects, fruit, some seeds

Hairy Woodpecker

Size 7 ½ inches (19 cm)
Habitat Woods, parks, orchards, suburbia
Breeds Alaska and forested Canada south to western Panama
Winters Resident in breeding range
Food Insects, berries, seeds, nuts

As

EASTERN KINGBIRD
Size 7 inches (18 cm)
Habitat Woodland edge, roadside fences
and wires, bushy areas, orchards, farms
Breeds Central Canada south to Gulf of
Mexico; rare in western North America
Winters Peru to Bolivia
Food Insects

As

EASTERN WOOD-PEWEE
Size 6 inches (15 cm)
Habitat Woodlands, parks
Breeds Southern Canada, eastern U.S.
Winters Costa Rica to Peru
Food Insects

As

EASTERN PHOEBE
Size 6 inches (15 cm)
Habitat Breeds in coniferous forest,
winters in wooded areas along streams,
roadsides, farms, suburbs
Breeds Eastern North America from
Canada to Gulf states
Winters Southern part of range to Mexico
Food Insects

J Juvenile   Feeds at birdtables   Feeds at hanging feeders   Uses nest boxes

TREE SWALLOW 🏠
Size 5 inches (13 cm)
Habitat Open areas near water, meadows, lakes
Breeds Alaska, Canada, much of eastern U.S.
Winters Southern U.S. to Central America
Food Flying insects

As

As

PURPLE MARTIN 🏠
Size 7 inches (18 cm)
Habitat Open country, farms, gardens; breeds in artificial martin houses
Breeds Southern Canada to Gulf States; less common in western regions
Winters South America
Food Flying insects

As

BARN SWALLOW
Size 6 inches (15 cm)
Habitat Farms, streamsides, meadows, parks
Breeds Most of North America
Winters Costa Rica to Argentina
Food Flying insects

Blue Jay

Size 10 inches (25 cm)
Habitat Oak and pine woods, suburbia
Breeds Eastern North America from southern Canada to Gulf states
Winters Resident in breeding range
Food Insects, seeds, nuts, berries, eggs, scraps

A*w*
A*s*

Tufted Titmouse

Size 5–6 inches (13–15 cm)
Habitat Woods, groves, gardens
Breeds Southern Ontario south to Gulf states
Winters Resident in breeding range
Food Seeds, nuts, insects

A*w*
A*s*

Black-capped form

Black-capped Chickadee

Size 4 ½ inches (11.5 cm)
Habitat Mixed and deciduous woods, thickets, gardens
Breeds Alaska, central and southern Canada, northern half of U.S.
Winters Resident, some southward movement in hard winters
Food Insects, seeds

A*w*
A*s*

A*w* A*s*

Carolina Chickadee

Size 4 ¼ inches (11 cm)
Habitat Woods, gardens, thickets
Breeds New Jersey, west to Kansas, south to Gulf Coast
Winters Resident
Food Insects, seeds

WHITE-BREASTED NUTHATCH 🏮 🏠
Size 5–6 inches (13–15 cm)
Habitat Forests, shelter belts, gardens with trees
Breeds Southern Canada to Mexico
Winters Resident in breeding range
Food Nuts, berries, seeds, insects

HOUSE WREN 🏠
Size 4–5 inches (10–13 cm)
Habitat Woods, thickets, gardens, parks
Breeds Southern Canada to Argentina
Winters Northern birds move into
   southern parts of range
Food Insects, spiders, small seeds

A*w*
A*s*

WINTER WREN
Size 3 ½–4 inches (9–10 cm)
Habitat Woods, gardens, parks, thickets
Breeds Southern Canada, Pacific states,
   northern U.S. east of Rocky Mountains
Winters Canada from southeast Alaska, Pacific
   states, southern half of eastern U.S.
Food Insects, spiders

A*w*
A*s*

GOLDEN-CROWNED KINGLET
Size 3 ½ inches (9 cm)
Habitat Coniferous woods, gardens
Breeds Southern Alaska and Canada
   south to North Carolina
Winters Southward to Gulf states
Food Insects, spiders

A*w*
A*s*

RUBY-CROWNED KINGLET
Aw As ♀

Size 4–5 inches (10–13 cm)
Habitat Conifers and mixed woodlands
Breeds Alaska, Canada, western U.S.,
    extreme northeastern U.S.
Winters To Gulf states, Central America
Food Insects, spiders

Aw
As
♂

AMERICAN REDSTART
Size 5 inches (13 cm)
Habitat Deciduous woods
Breeds Canada and eastern U.S.
Winters Mexico, West Indies, Brazil
Food Insects

As
♀

As ♂

YELLOW-RUMPED WARBLER 🐦
Size 5–6 inches (13–15 cm)
Habitat Coniferous and mixed woods, thickets
Breeds Alaska, Canada, south to Mexico in
    west and Tennessee in east
Winters Northeastern U.S., Pacific and
    Gulf coasts south to Panama
Food Insects

EASTERN BLUEBIRD 🏠
Size 6 inches (15 cm)
Habitat Scattered trees, parks, gardens
Breeds Eastern North America from southern
    Canada to Gulf states
Winters Northern birds move south in winter
Food Insects and other invertebrates, berries

As
♂

AMERICAN ROBIN

As ♂

Size 9–11 inches (23–28 cm)
Habitat Cities, towns, parks, gardens, open
woodland, orchards
Breeds North America, rarely nests in
north Florida
Winters Across U.S. and Central America
Food Worms, insects, berries, and fruit

BROWN THRASHER

Size 10½ inches (25 cm)
Habitat Thickets, shrubs
Breeds Southern Canada to Gulf states
Winters Resident in breeding range;
rare in western North America
Food Insects, fruits

As

CEDAR WAXWING

Aw
As
♂

Size 6 inches (15 cm)
Habitat Woodland, orchards, parks, gardens
Breeds Alaska, Canada to central U.S.
Winters From southern Canada south to Panama
Food Insects, berries

J

EUROPEAN STARLING

Size 8 inches (20 cm)
Habitat Cities, parks, farms, gardens
Breeds Southern Canada and whole of U.S.
Winters Across U.S., northern birds move south
Food Insects, worms, fruit, berries, seeds

As ♂

Key: ♂ Male ♀ Female **Aw** Adult winter **As** Adult summer

EASTERN TOWHEE

Size 7–8 inches (18–20 cm)
Habitat Open woods, undergrowth, gardens
Breeds Eastern North America from southern
    Canada to Florida
Winters Northerly breeding birds move south
Food Seeds, berries, insects

A*s* ♂

NORTHERN CARDINAL 🐦

Size 8–9 inches (20–23 cm)
Habitat Woodland edges, gardens, suburbia
Breeds Southern Ontario to Gulf States
    and southwestern U.S.
Winters Resident in breeding range
Food Fruit, berries, seeds, invertebrates

A*w* A*s* ♂

DARK-EYED JUNCO 🐦

Size 5 ¼–6 inches (14–17 cm)
Habitat Conifers and mixed woods, gardens,
    thickets, open ground in winter
Breeds Alaska, Canada, south in mountains to
    Arizona in the west, Georgia in the east
Winters South to Gulf States, Mexico
Food Insects, seeds, berries

A*s* ♀

WHITE-CROWNED SPARROW 🏮
Size 6 inches (15 cm)
Habitat Bushy places, roadsides, woodland edges
Breeds Alaska, Canada, western U.S.
Winters South to Gulf States, Mexico, Cuba
Food Seeds, insects

A*s*

A*w* A*s* ♂

BROWN-HEADED COWBIRD
Size 7 inches (18 cm)
Habitat Farms, fields, roadsides, woodland edges
Breeds Southern Canada to Mexico, northern Florida
Winters Northern birds move mainly to southern half of U.S.
Food Insects, fruits, grain, seeds

COMMON GRACKLE 🏮
Size 10-12 inches (25–30 cm)
Habitat Farms, towns, woodland edge
Breeds Central Canada through eastern U.S.
Winters Southern two-thirds of U.S. east of Rockies
Food Insects, invertebrates, fruit, berries

A*w*
A*s*
♂

Key: ♂ Male   ♀ Female   A*w* Adult winter   A*s* Adult summer

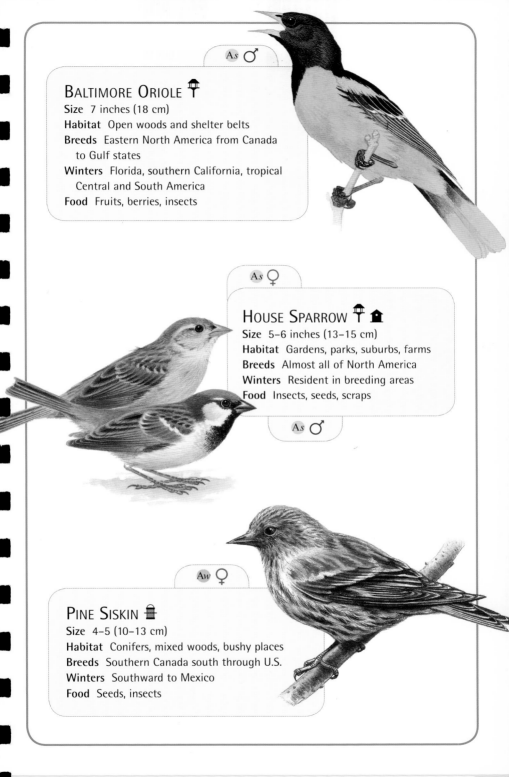

As ♂

Baltimore Oriole 🏠
Size 7 inches (18 cm)
Habitat Open woods and shelter belts
Breeds Eastern North America from Canada to Gulf states
Winters Florida, southern California, tropical Central and South America
Food Fruits, berries, insects

As ♀

House Sparrow 🏠 🏠
Size 5–6 inches (13–15 cm)
Habitat Gardens, parks, suburbs, farms
Breeds Almost all of North America
Winters Resident in breeding areas
Food Insects, seeds, scraps

As ♂

Aw ♀

Pine Siskin 🏠
Size 4–5 (10–13 cm)
Habitat Conifers, mixed woods, bushy places
Breeds Southern Canada south through U.S.
Winters Southward to Mexico
Food Seeds, insects

AMERICAN GOLDFINCH

Size 4–5 inches (10–13 cm)
Habitat Weedy places, gardens, parks, roadsides, woodland edges
Breeds Southern Canada and U.S. to northern Gulf states
Winters Canadian border through U.S. into northern Mexico
Food Seeds

A*s*

♂

PURPLE FINCH

Size 5–6 inches (13–15 cm)
Habitat Woods, groves, suburbs in winter
Breeds Canada, northeastern and western U.S.
Winters Widespread across U.S.
Food Seeds

A*s*

♂

HOUSE FINCH

Size 5–6 inches (13–15 cm)
Habitat Cities, suburbs, gardens, farms
Breeds Widespread in western U.S., spreading locally in east
Winters Resident in breeding areas
Food Seeds

A*s*

♂

EVENING GROSBEAK

Size 7–8 inches (18–20 cm)
Habitat Conifers, shrubs, gardens
Breeds Canada, western and northeastern U.S.
Winters Southward to Mexico
Food Seeds, fruits, berries

A*s*

♂

Key: 🕊 Feeds at birdtables   🕯 Feeds at hanging feeders   ♂ Male   A*s* Adult summer

BIRD LOGBOOK

This section is a logbook to help you keep track of your explorations and observations of the world of birds. There are pages for every week of the year, offering tips and prompts for recording birdlife and activity in your backyard or locality.

Important things to note include the date of the observations, the time, your location, perhaps the weather, and a list of the birds that you see. For more tips, refer to the chapter "Taking Notes and Making Sketches," on pages 72–75.

WEEK 1 starting __ / __ / __

SIGHTINGS

Species	No.	Food taken	Time	Weather

OBSERVATIONS

BIRD TRACKER TIP

If you see a bird you can't identify, don't jump to conclusions too quickly. Look carefully and check your identification book to see what is likely and what is not: the one that "looks right" at first glance in the pictures might not be found in your area or not at that time of year, so check the text too.

starting __ / __ / __

SIGHTINGS

Species	No.	Food taken	Time	Weather

OBSERVATIONS

WEEK 3　starting __ / __ / __

SIGHTINGS

Species	No.	Food taken	Time	Weather

OBSERVATIONS

BIRD TRACKER TIP

Try to learn the basic anatomy of your bird and its feather tracts. This will help you understand the bird's structural differences and its subsequent development. An understanding of the fundamentals, however vague, will enhance your awareness, and may help when you need to communicate with an expert in the field.

WEEK 4 starting __ / __ / __

SIGHTINGS

Species	No.	Food taken	Time	Weather

OBSERVATIONS

BIRD TRACKER TIP

Watch birds on the feeders and bird table and how they move around in your garden. They are remarkably quick: see how they take off from a bush, fly to the feeder, and "stop dead" when they reach it—small birds are almost insect-like in their stop-start movements and precision. Just think of the coordination between eyes, wings, and feet required to land on the side of a vertical nut basket.

WEEK 5 starting __ / __ / __

SIGHTINGS

Species	No.	Food taken	Time	Weather

OBSERVATIONS

BIRD TRACKER TIP

Birds use all kinds of signals to communicate: at a feeder, you will normally see aggression more than any other interaction. They use their voices but also visual signals, opening their wings and flattening their feathers to look big, wide, and impressive—an unmistakable "get out of my way or else." Such signals are there to avoid physical fighting, but you might see fierce fights over food, nevertheless.

WEEK 6 starting __ / __ / __

SIGHTINGS

Species	No.	Food taken	Time	Weather

OBSERVATIONS

BIRD TRACKER TIP

Keep an eye on the birds feeding outside your window: how many do you see at one time? You might have five or ten chickadees, but during the day, who knows how many will pass by? In many gardens, there might be five or ten times as many as this every day. Such a throughput might not be noticed unless the birds are individually marked with colored bands.

WEEK 7 starting __ / __ / __

SIGHTINGS

Species	No.	Food taken	Time	Weather

OBSERVATIONS

BIRD TRACKER TIP

Do all the birds feed in the same way around your feeders and bird table? Almost certainly there will be several different techniques and you can work out what is going on with a bit of close attention. Most birds eat at the table, or the feeder, but others take a nut or seed and fly off with it, to feed undisturbed nearby, or to store the food for later.

WEEK 8　starting ___ / ___ / ___

SIGHTINGS

Species	No.	Food taken	Time	Weather

OBSERVATIONS

BIRD TRACKER TIP

Birds must drink and bathe, even in the coldest weather, to keep themselves in good condition. Fresh, clean water is a lifeline for them, but it is difficult to keep it free from ice in winter. A floating ball might sometimes help: a tiny pump could be practical. But normally you just need to top it off regularly, and what you must never do is to use any kind of antifreeze additive.

WEEK 9 starting __ / __ / __

SIGHTINGS

Species	No.	Food taken	Time	Weather

OBSERVATIONS

BIRD TRACKER TIP

Some birds just don't feed on the food in hanging baskets or feeders and on tables. They just carry on in the same, natural way, feeding in the hedge or shrubs or on the ground underneath. You can help some of these species in bad weather by scattering grated cheese or other foods on the ground, under hedges and in flowerbeds, or even smearing fat in the crevices in tree bark.

WEEK 10 starting __ / __ / __

SIGHTINGS

Species	No.	Food taken	Time	Weather

OBSERVATIONS

BIRD TRACKER TIP

In spring, birds are looking for good nesting material. You can help them, and have a bit of extra amusement, if you put out bundles of straw, bits of wool, or even clumps of hair—from the dog, or even your own! A solid-wire basket is best to hold such material—avoid soft plastic mesh, and avoid long strands of cotton or other fiber that might entangle birds' legs.

WEEK 11 starting __ / __ / __

SIGHTINGS

Species	No.	Food taken	Time	Weather

OBSERVATIONS

BIRD TRACKER TIP

Many birds nest close to people. They are normally not especially prone to suffer from disturbance, but all the same, if you suspect a nest, it is best to avoid it if you can. It is usually safe to take a peek, but to do so at the wrong time might cause a bird to desert its eggs or chicks a day or two before they are ready.

WEEK 12 starting __ / __ / __

SIGHTINGS

Species	No.	Food taken	Time	Weather

OBSERVATIONS

BIRD TRACKER TIP

Look out for signs of woodpeckers on tree bark. Sometimes they chip away bits of bark or decaying wood to get at beetle larvae; sometimes they will drill small, round holes into smooth bark so that sticky sap oozes out; they return to feed on the sap and any insects that happen to get stuck in it. In North America, a small group of woodpeckers that habitually do this are known as sapsuckers.

WEEK 13 starting __ / __ / __

SIGHTINGS

Species	No.	Food taken	Time	Weather

OBSERVATIONS

BIRD TRACKER TIP

Try to learn a bird song or call each week. It is always best to match the sound with the bird by following up the call and seeing exactly what is making it: then fix it in your mind. You might make up a word or phrase that is suggestive of the rhythm or pattern of the sound that will help you to recall it later.

WEEK 14 starting __ / __ / __

SIGHTINGS

Species	No.	Food taken	Time	Weather

OBSERVATIONS

BIRD TRACKER TIP

Check your binoculars now and then: look at the individual eyepiece adjustment to make sure it has not moved from your ideal position. We all have a different balance between our eyes, so it is important to get the adjustment right and keep it right. Clean the lenses, blowing away dust or crumbs before you do any wiping with a soft, clean cloth.

WEEK 15 starting __ / __ / __

SIGHTINGS

Species	No.	Food taken	Time	Weather

OBSERVATIONS

BIRD TRACKER TIP

Try photographing your local birds: they are as challenging, and rewarding, as any other wildlife subject. Try to get some action and atmosphere into your pictures. The perfect, static, beautifully lit, and sharply focused portrait is something to aim for, but everyone does that—why not be different?

WEEK 16 starting __ / __ / __

SIGHTINGS

Species	No.	Food taken	Time	Weather

144

OBSERVATIONS

WEEK 17 starting __ / __ / __

SIGHTINGS

Species	No.	Food taken	Time	Weather

OBSERVATIONS

BIRD TRACKER TIP

If you have any ability at all, sketching birds is really rewarding: but it is not easy. They do not stay still for long. Just sketch while you can, fast and loose, and if the bird flies off, start on the next. Just keep doing it until you get more confident and begin to capture the birds' expressions and character.

WEEK 18 starting __ / __ / __

SIGHTINGS

Species	No.	Food taken	Time	Weather

OBSERVATIONS

BIRD TRACKER TIP

If you draw birds, try to draw what you see in front of you rather than what you know about from other sources. Details of the feet, all the outlines of the feathers—these are things that you may have seen in a book, but most of the time you can't see them when observing birds, so why draw them? Get real: put in what you see and nothing else and your pictures will come alive.

WEEK 19 starting __ / __ / __

SIGHTINGS

Species	No.	Food taken	Time	Weather

OBSERVATIONS

BIRD TRACKER TIP

If you put out peanuts to feed birds, keep them chopped up in tiny pieces, or put them in a small-mesh basket so that the nuts last longer. This would also prevent the occasional rare incidence of a baby bird choking on a large peanut given by its parent.

WEEK 20 starting __ / __ / __

SIGHTINGS

Species	No.	Food taken	Time	Weather

OBSERVATIONS

BIRD TRACKER TIP

A nest box can work well in a garden, but do not be tempted to put out too many for the size of the garden. Most birds are territorial and too many boxes in a small area are likely to cause birds to spend all day fighting each other instead of rearing their young. Keep boxes away from feeders, too: nesting birds need peace and seclusion.

WEEK 21 starting __ / __ / __

SIGHTINGS

Species	No.	Food taken	Time	Weather

OBSERVATIONS

BIRD TRACKER TIP

If you are a gardener, consider the wildlife when you are planting up a new border or patch of ground. Search the Internet for details of native plants in your area and match what you use to your soil; remember that flowers with an abundance of nectar are good for insects, which are good for birds. In North America, flowers with abundant nectar are also good for hummingbirds.

WEEK 22 starting __ / __ / __

SIGHTINGS

Species	No.	Food taken	Time	Weather

OBSERVATIONS

BIRD TRACKER TIP

If you have space, a garden pond is a great idea. It should be situated away from hedges and trees that would fill it with leaves in fall. Dig twice the depth you need, then add a piece of old carpet, a rubber or plastic pond liner, and some soil. Be careful not to use non-native water plants, which could germinate elsewhere and cause havoc in local streams.

WEEK 23 starting __ / __ / __

SIGHTINGS

Species	No.	Food taken	Time	Weather

OBSERVATIONS

BIRD TRACKER TIP

If you have a pond, make sure at least part of its edge is shallow and shelves smoothly up to dry ground. That way, even the smaller birds can walk in and bathe or drink, without having to dive into deep water. A few well-placed stones around the edge will help to keep open spaces between clumps of vegetation.

WEEK 24 starting __ / __ / __

SIGHTINGS

Species	No.	Food taken	Time	Weather

OBSERVATIONS

BIRD TRACKER TIP

If you visit the seashore or marsh, make sure you check the times of the tides, both for your own safety and as a guide to bird activity. Shore birds are often resting in a protected place at high tide, while at low tide they come out in numbers to feed in exposed areas.

WEEK 25 starting __ / __ / __

SIGHTINGS

Species	No.	Food taken	Time	Weather

OBSERVATIONS

BIRD TRACKER TIP

A vacation is a great time to see new birds in different habitats. Get used to using a topographic map: good maps are mines of information of value to the nature-watcher. Find appropriate habitats, such as woods, streams, lakes, and marshes, and good vantage points that will give you an extensive view with the sun behind you at the right time of day.

WEEK 26 starting __ / __ / __

SIGHTINGS

Species	No.	Food taken	Time	Weather

OBSERVATIONS

BIRD TRACKER TIP

Baby birds that seem to be "abandoned" are always best left alone, as their parents will invariably be nearby. If a bird is obviously sick or injured, do not try to look after it yourself. Most towns and cities in the U.S. have bird rehabilitators nearby and birders should make a point of learning who they are. Paying them a visit may allow you to see birds up close that are sometimes difficult to see.

SIGHTINGS

Species	No.	Food taken	Time	Weather

OBSERVATIONS

BIRD TRACKER TIP

If only once, you should make a point of getting up very early and going to a local woodland to listen to the dawn chorus: it is remarkable and moving, something that can hardly be described but has to be experienced firsthand for the full, spectacular effect to be properly appreciated.

WEEK 28 starting  __ / __ / __

SIGHTINGS

Species	No.	Food taken	Time	Weather

OBSERVATIONS

BIRD TRACKER TIP

Water is always a bonus on any bird-watching trip: try to find a good lake, reservoir, or flooded pit and you will undoubtedly enjoy a great variety of species, some of them probably best appreciated at close range. A quiet summer evening is a lovely time to visit such a place.

WEEK 29 starting __ / __ / __

SIGHTINGS

Species	No.	Food taken	Time	Weather

170

OBSERVATIONS

BIRD TRACKER TIP

Some migrants begin to move south surprisingly early, in late summer or early fall. It is always easy to take note of the first migrant you see in spring but much less so to notice the last of any species that you see in the year. Keeping notes of such observations will help you anticipate future movements of various species.

WEEK 30 starting  __ / __ / __

SIGHTINGS

Species	No.	Food taken	Time	Weather

OBSERVATIONS

BIRD TRACKER TIP

Migrating wading birds can turn up at the edge of a pool almost anywhere in spring and fall. To see them locally you may need to return to a suitable watery habitat many times, as some may stay for days but others may be present for only a few hours.

WEEK 31 starting __ / __ / __

SIGHTINGS

Species	No.	Food taken	Time	Weather

OBSERVATIONS

_____

_____

_____

_____

_____

_____

_____

_____

_____

_____

_____

_____

_____

_____

_____

_____

_____

BIRD TRACKER TIP

Bird guides on video and DVD show aspects of birds' movement and song and DVD guides can also carry large amounts of other information. Use these sources in combination with the precision and portability of your pocket guidebook, which is unbeatable for quick reference while you are watching birds.

WEEK 32 starting __ / __ / __

SIGHTINGS

Species	No.	Food taken	Time	Weather

OBSERVATIONS

BIRD TRACKER TIP

Listen for migrants passing overhead at night. There is no point spending hours outside doing this, but if you are outside after dark, be aware that some birds might be passing overhead and listen for them. It is surprising what unexpected calls might be heard even over urban areas during migration periods.

WEEK 33 starting __ / __ / __

SIGHTINGS

Species	No.	Food taken	Time	Weather

OBSERVATIONS

BIRD TRACKER TIP

Television weather forecasts are an excellent resource for bird-watchers, especially detailed forecasts with proper synoptic charts. It can be possible to predict "good days" when it is worth traveling to the coast or a migration watch point—especially if there is a clear night with tail winds, which is good for migration, followed by poor weather, cloud, or fog, which forces birds to land.

WEEK 34 starting __ / __ / __

SIGHTINGS

Species	No.	Food taken	Time	Weather

OBSERVATIONS

WEEK 35 starting __ / __ / __

SIGHTINGS

Species	No.	Food taken	Time	Weather

OBSERVATIONS

BIRD TRACKER TIP

Wet weather can be good for birds but is not so good for watching them. A blind gives good shelter, but even good, breathable, waterproof fabrics may not make a day out in the rain especially comfortable. Don't neglect the old-fashioned umbrella—with a hooked handle to curl under one arm, it can be a great help.

WEEK 36 starting __ / __ / __

SIGHTINGS

Species	No.	Food taken	Time	Weather

OBSERVATIONS

BIRD TRACKER TIP

Migrant birds need plenty of nutritious food to give them a high-energy intake for the least amount of effort. Bushes with juicy, sugar-rich berries strongly attract some species of migrant warblers, concentrating local populations into the best feeding areas—if you can find these areas, you will see a lot of birds.

WEEK 37 starting __ / __ / __

SIGHTINGS

Species	No.	Food taken	Time	Weather

OBSERVATIONS

BIRD TRACKER TIP

Be aware of your behavior and surroundings when you are out in the countryside—
if you want to see birds, you must keep quiet. Approach the edges of habitats,
streams, and rivers with special care, looking both ways to try to see birds before
they see you.

WEEK 38 starting __ / __ / __

SIGHTINGS

Species	No.	Food taken	Time	Weather

OBSERVATIONS

WEEK 39 starting __ / __ / __

SIGHTINGS

Species	No.	Food taken	Time	Weather

OBSERVATIONS

BIRD TRACKER TIP

Look at birds' plumages in fall and see how, if at all, their colors and patterns differ between seasons, with age, or between male and female. With small birds up close—as at the kitchen window—or big birds in the countryside, it is fascinating to see the progress of their fall molt, as gaps appear and fill again in their feathers.

WEEK 40 starting __ / __ / __

SIGHTINGS

Species	No.	Food taken	Time	Weather

OBSERVATIONS

BIRD TRACKER TIP

When in the countryside, all bird-watchers should respect the welfare of birds, domestic and other animals, and the rights of other people and landowners. Observe practices such as not leaving litter, closing gates, and clearing up after your dog, if you have one.

WEEK 41 starting __ / __ / __

SIGHTINGS

Species	No.	Food taken	Time	Weather

OBSERVATIONS

BIRD TRACKER TIP

Cats can be a menace in a bird-watcher's garden. Various pellets and liquid deterrents may help keep dogs and cats away, but many are determined and not so easily put off. An electronic cat deterrent, which gives an ultrasound bleep when triggered, can be more effective, and does no harm to the neighbors' pets.

WEEK 42 starting  __ / __ / __

SIGHTINGS

Species	No.	Food taken	Time	Weather

OBSERVATIONS

BIRD TRACKER TIP

You may see birds that simply don't look like anything you have in your books. These may be "escapes," such as parrots, finches, weavers, and other cage birds, that have been released or have escaped and managed to survive for a time. Others are simply aberrant in some way, such as albinos, piebald leucistic birds (which have an excess of white), or abnormally pale individuals with reduced feather pigment.

WEEK 43 starting __ / __ / __

SIGHTINGS

Species	No.	Food taken	Time	Weather

OBSERVATIONS

_____

_____

_____

_____

_____

_____

_____

_____

_____

_____

_____

_____

BIRD TRACKER TIP

If you want to watch birds with other people, try visiting a nature reserve and joining an organized walk with the guide. You could also join a local bird club or group and go on their trips.

WEEK 44 starting __ / __ / __

SIGHTINGS

Species	No.	Food taken	Time	Weather

OBSERVATIONS

BIRD TRACKER TIP

For a good idea of how different species of birds get along in the same area or habitat, go to a tidal beach and watch the shorebirds. Wading birds with different lengths of leg and bill, or different bill shapes, feed on different foods, some in water, some in mud, some on sand, some picking from the surface, some probing more deeply.

WEEK 45 starting __ / __ / __

SIGHTINGS

Species	No.	Food taken	Time	Weather

OBSERVATIONS

BIRD TRACKER TIP

Like shorebirds, ducks have a great variety of behavior: some dive, feeding on animal matter or plant matter; others graze on dry land; others dabble in the shallow water at the edge of a lake. Some species seem to be constantly active by day, others sleep, feeding mostly at night. They are worth watching to try to gain a better understanding of how variety can be supported in a small area.

WEEK 46 starting  __ / __ / __

SIGHTINGS

Species	No.	Food taken	Time	Weather

OBSERVATIONS

WEEK 47 starting __ / __ / __

SIGHTINGS

Species	No.	Food taken	Time	Weather

OBSERVATIONS

BIRD TRACKER TIP

How many birds hang around your house or the office building, or sit around on roofs in town, but hardly seem to come to the ground? It is interesting to watch town and suburban birds and see just where they feed and what they do all day. Gulls and crows might appear to stand on the roof or the television antenna all day long, but they obviously do come down to eat somewhere, sometime—see if you can find out more.

WEEK 48 starting __ / __ / __

SIGHTINGS

Species	No.	Food taken	Time	Weather

OBSERVATIONS

BIRD TRACKER TIP

Listen for very quiet bird song. Sometimes a bird will sing—as if "singing to itself" or "daydreaming"—so quietly that you have to be very close to hear it. The song may be like normal song or quite different. This type of singing is known as subsong: it occurs often in young birds learning their genetically programmed species repertoire or in adult birds early in the breeding season.

WEEK 49 starting __ / __ / __

SIGHTINGS

Species	No.	Food taken	Time	Weather

OBSERVATIONS

BIRD TRACKER TIP

If you get a fall of snow, look for tracks and other signs of birds and other wildlife. Birds may leave telltale marks, such as the sweep of wingtips made by a hawk diving on its prey, or the giant footprints of a heron coming unsuspected to your garden pond at dawn. Mud is a fair substitute.

WEEK 50 starting __ / __ / __

SIGHTINGS

Species	No.	Food taken	Time	Weather

OBSERVATIONS

BIRD TRACKER TIP

If you find feathers, try to identify which species and which part of the body they came from. The distinctive stiff quills of flight and tail feathers are quite unlike the softer contour feathers of the body. A shed feather reveals unexpected patterns, too, as spots and bars become apparent on the inner edge that are usually hidden on the living bird.

WEEK 51 starting __ / __ / __

SIGHTINGS

Species	No.	Food taken	Time	Weather

OBSERVATIONS

BIRD TRACKER TIP

As you build up bird diaries or notebooks, it is useful to compare a past year's notes with the current year to see whether the bird life in your area has changed in any way. Are there more or fewer birds of certain species? Did they come and go earlier or later this year? Half the fun of keeping notes is to compare them over time.

WEEK 52 starting  __ / __ / __

SIGHTINGS

Species	No.	Food taken	Time	Weather

OBSERVATIONS

BIRD TRACKER TIP

There's no harm looking at the bird-watching year and trying to plan what to do next year, to see the highlights over again or to get to see new ones. A year goes quickly and fitting in all the birds you would like to see is barely possible. Identify a few gaps now, and think about how, when, and where you might fill them in the year to come.

GLOSSARY

abrasion Wear and tear on feathers, often removing paler spots and fringes and fading darker colors.

albinism A lack of pigment: true albinos are white with pink eyes, but most "white" birds are partial albinos, or albinistic, with patches of white and normal eye colors.

axillaries The feathers under the base of the wing, in the "wingpit." Also known as axillars.

band A metal band placed around a bird's leg, with an individual number; when the bird is caught or found dead, its movements can be traced. Also known as a ring.

bastard wing A tuft of feathers on the "thumb," halfway along the leading edge of the wing, which can be raised or lowered to control airflow in flight. Also called the alula.

beak Synonymous with bill; the two jaws and their horny covering.

binocular vision The ability to see an area with both eyes; birds such as owls have forward-facing eyes, giving the greatest extent of binocular vision.

bird of prey Usually refers to daytime birds of prey, including eagles, vultures, hawks, falcons, harriers, and kites; may be used to include owls. Also called "raptors," or raptorial birds.

blind A small shelter from which to observe birds while remaining hidden from view. Also known as a hide.

brood A set of young birds hatched from one clutch of eggs.

call note A vocalization, usually characteristic of the species, made to maintain contact, warn of danger, or for other specific purposes.

cap A patch of color on the top of a bird's head, usually on the feathers of the forehead and crown.

carpal joint The bend of the wing, at the "wrist."

chick A young bird before it is able to fly.

clutch A set of eggs laid and incubated together in the nest; if these are lost, a replacement clutch may be laid; some species have several clutches during the course of one breeding season, others ("single brooded") have only one.

colony A group of nests close together, often on the ground (e.g., gulls and terns) or in trees (e.g., herons).

color ring or band A plastic or metal band placed on a bird's leg; a combination of colors or numbers on the band allow individual recognition without having to capture the bird.

corvid A bird of the crow family or corvidae.

courtship Usually ritualized behavior, male and female together forming a pair bond before breeding.

cryptic Describes coloration that gives a bird camouflage or makes it harder to see.

dawn chorus The loud chorus of bird song heard in spring from just before dawn, especially in woodland.

display A form of ritualized behavior with a specific function, for example in courtship, or in distracting potential predators.

distribution The geographical range of a species, often split into breeding range, wintering range, and areas in which it may be seen on migration.

drake A male duck (females are then "ducks").

drumming The sound made in spring by a woodpecker vibrating its bill against a branch; also made by a snipe diving through the air with outer tail feathers extended and vibrating.

dusting "Bathing" in loose, dry sand, dust, or soil to help remove parasites from feathers.

eclipse A dull plumage worn by male ducks and geese in summer.

extinct Describes a species no longer living anywhere on Earth; if a species has disappeared from a country or region, but is still found elsewhere, it is properly described as having been "extirpated" from that area.

fall A sudden large arrival of migrant birds, especially when caused by bad weather on the coast.

feral Describes a bird or species that has escaped from captivity to live wild.

field "In the field" means "in the wild" or out of doors (as opposed to being captive, or held "in the hand").

field guide An identification guide to birds as they are seen wild and free.

field of view The extent of the area that can be seen through a telescope or binoculars at a given distance, expressed in degrees (angular field of view) or distance (linear field of view); higher magnification typically results in a smaller field of view.

fledgling A young bird that has just learned to fly and has its first covering of feathers.

flock A group of birds behaving in some sort of unison: tight flocks (e.g., starlings in flight) are obvious, but loose, feeding flocks of birds in woodland may be less so.

game bird Usually used to describe one of the pheasant, partridge, grouse, or quail families—other birds commonly shot for sport include ducks and geese ("waterfowl").

genus A category in classification above species, indicating close relationships. Appears as the first word in a two- or three-word scientific name (e.g., *homo* in *homo sapiens*, or *falco* in *falco peregrinus*). Plural is "genera."

gorget Band of color or pattern, such as streaks, around the bird's upper breast.

habitat The environment that a species requires for survival. Its characteristics include shelter, water, food, feeding areas, nest sites, and roosting sites. More loosely described in such terms as "lowland heath" or "deciduous woodland"; also used for particular times of year or types of behavior, e.g., muddy estuary, open sea, ploughed fields.

hen A female bird.

immature Describes a bird not yet old enough to breed or have full adult plumage colors.

incubation Maintenance of proper temperature of the egg to allow development of the embryo.

jizz A kind of indefinable quality that gives a species a character of its own, combining shape, color, and—especially—actions.

juvenile The young bird in its first full plumage. Also known as juvenal in the U.S.

loafing Sitting or standing, often in groups, apparently doing little or nothing. Gulls, for example, "loaf" for hours at a time.

mandible The jaw and its horny sheath; upper and lower mandibles together form the beak or bill.

measurements The size of a bird is usually indicated by the length from bill tip to tail tip on a bird laid out on a flat surface. In reality, the apparent "size" depends as much on shape and bulk as on simple length.

migration A regular, seasonal movement of birds from one region or continent to another, between alternate areas occupied at different times of year.

molt The replacement of a bird's feathers, in a regular sequence characteristic of each species. There may be a complete molt or a partial molt depending on the season.

nest A receptacle built to take a clutch of eggs and, in many species, the young birds before they are able to fly; eggs may also be laid on a bare ledge or on the ground, with no nest structure being made.

nocturnal Active at night.

numbers Bird populations vary hugely from season to season, so are best described in terms of a particular measure that is easily repeated, usually "breeding pairs." In the case of large, more easily counted birds, such as ducks and geese, the measure is the total number of individuals at a certain season.

ornithology The study of birds: usually refers to scientific study of biology and ecology, while the hobby of watching birds is known simply as bird-watching or birding.

passage migrant A species or bird seen in some intermediate area during its migration from summer to winter quarters (or vice versa).

passerine A "perching bird."

plumage A covering of feathers; also often used to describe the overall colors and patterns of the feathers, defining a bird's appearance according to age, sex, and season.

preening Care of the feathers, especially using the bill to "zip" the structures back into place.

race A recognizable geographical group, or subspecies, within a species. Often there is no obvious border between groups, which blend (in a "cline") from one extreme to another. There may be more distinctive differences between isolated areas, such as islands, in which case the decision whether there are races, or separate species, can be difficult.

rarity An individual bird in an area where it is not normally seen, or is seen in only very small numbers. A species with a small world population is "rare."

roost To sleep; also the area where birds sleep.

scapulars A bunch of feathers on the shoulder.

seabird A species that comes to land to nest, but otherwise lives at sea and is not normally seen inland.

soaring Flight, often at a high level, in which the wings are held almost still, using air currents for lift and propulsion.

song A vocalization with a specific purpose and usually distinctive for each species: in particular, advertising the presence of a bird on its territory.

species A group, or groups, of individuals that can produce fertile young. Different species rarely interbreed naturally; if they do so, infertile hybrid offspring are produced.

territory An area defended for exclusive use by an individual bird or a family. Both breeding and winter-feeding territories may be defended.

twitcher A bird-watcher temporarily engaged in "twitching" (hearing of the presence of an individual rare bird and traveling with the intention of seeing it). Not then, despite the media's frequent incorrect usage, a bird-watcher, but a particular kind of bird-watcher.

wader A plover, sandpiper, curlew, or related species; in North America, usually called a "shorebird." Since some do not wade and some do not live on the shore, neither word is entirely satisfactory.

waterfowl Ducks, geese, and swans. Also known as wildfowl.

FURTHER RESOURCES

BOOKS:
Every bird-watcher needs a good bird identification book, or field guide. Guides that contain photographs can be helpful, but the number of illustrations may be restricted, especially for those species with different plumages according to age, sex, and season. A field guide with excellent illustrations has several advantages over a photographic guide. The birds are all in an ideal position, usually sideways, all nicely lit with no shadows or spots of sunlight to distract you from the true color of the bird. A book that tells you where to watch birds—in your local area, or across the country—can also be helpful. Other books can teach you about bird behavior—a "handbook" will usually give details of their habitats, migrations, food, eggs, and so on.

Dunne, Peter. *The Feather Quest: A North American Birder's Year.* Wilmington: Mariner Books, 1999.
Elbroch, Mark. *Bird Tracks and Signs: A Guide to North American Species.* Mechanicsburg: Stackpole Books, 2001.
Hall, Derek (editor). *Encyclopedia of North American Birds: An Essential Guide to Common Birds of North America.* San Diego: Thunder Bay Press, 2004.
Kessler, Brad. *Birds in Fall: A Novel.* New York: Scribner, 2007.
Sibley, David. *The North American Bird Guide.* Mountfield: Pica, 2000.
Sibley, David. *National Audubon Society: The Sibley Guide to Bird Life and Behavior.* New York: Knopf, 2001.
Sibley, David. *The Sibley Field Guide to the Birds of Eastern North America.* New York: Knopf, 2003.
Wheeler, Brian K. and Clark, William S. *A Photographic Guide to North American Raptors.* Princeton: Princeton University Press, 2003.

WEB SITES:
Web sites fall into several categories: bird-chat or "forum" type, the information source, the photographer's shop window, the environmentalist, and the holiday tour report.

www.americanbirding.org
The Web site for the American Birding Association, the only organization in North America that caters to recreational birders.

www.audubon.org
The National Audubon Society, established in 1905, is a leading environmental organization dedicated to conservancy.

www.birds.cornell.edu/AllAboutBirds
Contains a huge amount of detailed information on American birds.

www.birdlife.org
The site for BirdLife International, the global partnership of conservation organizations.

www.iucnredlist.org
The IUCN Red List of Threatened Species.

www.aou.org
The Web site of the American Ornithologists' Union, the largest group in the Americas devoted to the scientific study of birds.

www.bto.org/birdfacts
Has information on different bird species, including basic details of birds' lifestyles.

www.naturecanada.ca
Nature Canada (BirdLife's partner in Canada)

www.rspb.org.uk
The Royal Society for the Protection of Birds site opens up to 14,000 pages of detailed information: simply log on and explore.

www.birdsaustralia.com.au
Birds Australia (BirdLife's Australian partner)

MAGAZINES:
You can get birding magazines with club or society memberships, or by subscription, or from bookstores. Subscription magazines may be more specialized, and there are many scientific journals for the advanced bird enthusiast. Try a few—visit a library or bird club meeting, and talk to other bird-watchers.

Cornell Lab of Ornithology publishes two magazines: *Living Bird* (the Lab's award-winning magazine) and *BirdScope* (their newsletter).

World Birdwatch is BirdLife's International magazine—crammed with recent news and authoritative articles about birds, their habitats, and bird conservation around the world.

INDEX

ACKNOWLEDGEMENTS

Photography: François Gohier/Ardea (p10); Andrew Syred/Science Photo Library (p16)

Illustrations: Norman Arlott, Dianne Breeze, Keith Brewer, Hilary Burn, Chris Christoforou, Richard Draper, Malcolm Ellis, Mark Franklin, Robert Gillmor, Peter Hayman, Gary Hincks, Aziz Khan, Colin Newman, Denys Ovenden, David Quinn, Andrew Robinson, Chris Rose, David Thelwell, Gill Tomblin, Owen Williams, Ann Winterbotham, Ken Wood, and Michael Woods.